More Praise for
Love, Judy

"*Love, Judy* is personal, poignant, sometimes humorous nitty-gritty front line commentary from a woman in the midst of surviving breast cancer and the treatment for it. . . . [*Love, Judy*] is a book of hope and healing for women who share her diagnosis and for those who share their journey."
—Jean Shinoda Bolen, M.D.
author of *Goddesses in Everywoman* and *Crossing to Avalon*

"*Love, Judy* uses humor and a never-ending enthusiasm for life to bring the reader gently into the world of a woman battling breast cancer. . . . demonstrates how we are both vulnerable and able in grappling with life-threatening situations and how finding an active stance can help us heal and grow."
—*Common Ground*

"Judy Hart offers such pure 'essence' of personal rituals for healing."
—Jeanne Achterberg, Ph.D.
author of *Rituals of Healing* and *Woman as Healer*

"[Judy is] frank and humorous, supportive and gentle. Her insights into the battle of breast cancer possess a quality of understanding that takes her words into the lives of all women struggling to find an active response to healing and growing. . . . reading *Love, Judy* feels like the wonderful gift of friendship."
—*NAPRA Trade Journal*

"Warm, supportive and humorous."
—Susan Mayall, *Goodenough Books*

Love, Judy

Letters of Hope and Healing
For Women with Breast Cancer

Judy Hart

Conari Press
Berkeley, CA

To John,
With love,
For our twenty-six years of marriage,
And his steadfastness through my cancers.

Portions of this book have previously appeared in *The Folio, A Journal for Focusing and Experiential Therapy* and *The Focusing Connection*.

Printed in the United States of America on recycled paper
Cover: Fassino Design
Illustrations: Christine Leech

ISBN: 0-943233-52-6

Conari Press books are distributed by Publishers Group West

Library of Congress Cataloging-in-Publication Data

Hart, Judy, 1937-
    Love, Judy : letters of hope and healing for women with breast cancer / Judy Hart.
        p.   cm.
    ISBN 0-943233-52-6 : $10.95
    1. Breast—Cancer—Psychological aspects. 2. Healing. 3. Self-care, Health. I. Title.
RC280.B8H38   1993
616.99′449—dc20   93-26701
                                                                                          CIP

Table of Contents

Acknowledgments

A very special appreciation to Hank Hoey, Ph.D., for his skillful and compassionate shepherding, and for accompanying me on the therapeutic voyage of the psyche that long preceded my diagnosis and made all the difference in how I met cancer.

To all the recipients of the original cancer letters: especially my caring and extensive family—sisters, cousins, their families, and my family-in-law—and my many loving friends and neighbors, and also to medical support people, cancer patients and veterans, and unknown friends of friends, for powerful support of me as a cancer patient and generous responses to me as the writer of these letters.

To my savvy, humane, and humor-loving bevy of doctors: Norman Cohen, Anthony Engelbrecht, and Bob Fowler, aimiable strategists on the front line of defense; Alan Greenbaum and Debra Levinsky, dear old faithfuls adding further cheerful participation and support; Walter Rolfing, Robert Swanson, and Jeffery Wolf in important cameo roles; and their welcoming, reassuring, office staffs.

To the resourceful staff of 4NE, and particularly my most frequent oncology nurses during my seven stays at Alta Bates Medical Center: Betty Ajero, Tammy

Baltic, Carolyn Berson, Barbara Deem, Carol Dodson, Shirley Fontenot, Suzanne Gooding, Claire Hauser, Martha Johnston, Mari Kalishock, Judy McKay, Dennis Orme, Lene Pederson, Chris Petzoldt, Linda Pickering, Gretchen Seccombe, Tanja Schlosser, Carol Smith, Nancy Velasco, and Cheryl Willin. Also to Patti Pattison, Administrative Director of Clinical Nursing, and Nancee Hirano, Bone Marrow Transplant Clinical Nurse Specialist. And to all the staff of 6N, particularly my most frequent surgery care nurses, Erna Berg and Dottie Kohn.

To the many other individuals—staff and volunteers—throughout Alta Bates Medical Center, who cared for me in so many ways, particularly the people in Surgery, Pre-Op Testing, Admittance, X-Ray, Nuclear Medicine, Pheresis, Utilization Review, and the Business Office.

To the spirited and gentle technologists and staff of the Radiation Oncology Department of Summit Medical Center, who know what a sense of humor is, and particularly to my most frequent caregivers: Edward Millner, Karen Prins, Mary Rodigou, George Sanchez, and Lisa Wanket.

To every single member of the compassionate and personable staff of the Comprehensive Cancer Center, whose warm reception at my frequent checkups makes me feel that our human connection is as important as our medical purpose.

To the friendly staffs of Berkeley Internal Medicine and Huntmont Labs for smoothing my way with warm exchanges.

To Karen Burt-Imira, M.D., Carol Erickson, M.S.C.C., and Bob Avenson, Ph.D., for powerful healing hypnotic voyages during and after treatment.

To Pepper Sbarbaro, R.N., Trager practitioner, Scott Maloney, L.Ac., and

Raymond Biase, D.C., for kindly adjunctive physical care to my beleagured body, and to Ray's staff, who always found a way to squeeze me in.

To Carolyn Aldigé, President of the Cancer Research Foundation of America and the many readers of CRFA's *Monitor*—so numerous I could never get them on the letter list--who showered me with get well cards throughout my treatment.

To members of the Focusing Community for our shared appreciation of inner process, for Focusing sessions exchanged during and after treatment, and for responding vigorously and imaginatively at the 1992 Shenoa Retreat to my invitation to do "Silly Walks."

To the participants in my writing groups for cancer patients and post-treatment veterans, and other cancer patients who have shared their experiences and feelings, including groups at The Women's Cancer Resource Center in Berkeley and The Wellness Community in Walnut Creek.

To fellow writers, Mona Halaby and Elizabeth Fishel, to the members of Elizabeth's writing classes, to Ann Weiser Cornell, Focusing teacher, and to Diane Burnside for their invaluable feedback on parts of the manuscript. To Alice Adams, who, in my earliest writing days, helped me to know that I was a writer.

To friends who played a part in the production of the original cancer letters: Pat Day, who made a computer mailing list and labels; Wanda Nusted, who helped me select rubber stamp images to highlight the text on the original letters, took the letters to photocopy when I was not up to it, helped stuff envelopes, and also created the eight imaginative hats that I wore through treatment. To Jenny Holck, who, along with Wanda, contributed ideas for graphics for the book.

To Richard, Wilda, and Ann Flower, and to Susan and Brian Mayall for loans of their writer's dreamhouses in secluded, beautiful spots where parts of the book were written.

To Tiffany Cain and Cecilia Delgado and her family, who took on the cleaning of my house through treatment and added cheer by their presence.

To Kathi Jaramillo for research assistance on the book proposal and Kathleen Dunbar for creating order out of the chaos of information and papers as I wrote the book.

To Judy and Matt McKay, Janice Greenberg, and Julie Bennett for leading me to Conari Press.

To Mary Jane Ryan, editor supreme for her sensitivity and respect for my voice as a writer, and other denizens of Conari Press—Karen Bouris, Emily Miles, Will Glennon, and David Wells for their good work and for educating me about the publishing process.

To all the other people not mentioned above who helped me through cancer or on the book, whether over time or in a single meaningful gesture or encounter.

And finally, to the Human Psyche and her magical contributions to the healing process.

About the Book

As you read these words, I welcome you into a healing environment. In my two unrelated breast cancers, I invited a healing atmosphere to form around and inside me. Now I invite you into this friendly place which is both concrete and a powerful product of the imagination.

This book is made up of two alternating sets of letters: the ten original ones I wrote, photocopied, and sent through ten months of treatment for my second breast cancer (they went to about three hundred people—family, friends, neighbors, acquaintances, an ever-growing community of medical people, and cancer patients who heard about the letters from friends); the ten letters I've written over the past year directly to you, the reader of this book; and a final letter, written two years after diagnosis, addressed to all of you.

My original letters share not only the moments of shock, of just "hanging in there," and of triumphs, but also detailed accounts of my healing activities: self-hypnosis, imagery, Focusing sessions, affirmations, dreams, self-support writings, humor, my musings on healing, and relating to the many people in my path. These letters brought tremendous support from my readers, which gave me a sense of community. Now you can share in the power of that well-wishing community.

As you read my story, I hope you'll feel less alone and find comfort in similarities of feeling and experience. You will also find differences. Please remember that each person's combination of body, cancer, treatment, personality, and circumstances is different, so you need not assume that a particular moment or treatment will be the same for you as it was for me. It may be particularly helpful to recall this if you read that something was hard for me and fear that therefore it will be for you, or if you have a hard time with something that seemed not to be so for me. Despite the inevitable differences, I hope you will benefit from this connection with someone who has been through breast cancer and is rooting for you.

My letters to you are my reaching out to encourage you on your healing journey, *which is uniquely yours*, and offer suggestions that are both concrete and open-ended for helping yourself through and after treatment. There is enough guidance in these letters to be a "how-to," but if, like me, you find most "how-to's" too rigid, know that you can also gain just by letting the material wash over you or by adapting ideas and attitudes to your needs and style.

Each letter to you is a topic complete in itself, so you can read one that feels pertinent at a given moment without having read everything up to that point. The themes in "your" letters also run through the original letters to my friends, and I have tried to place each topic after the original letter in which it came up. The annotated Table of Contents is designed to help you find subjects you want as well as avoid those that might feel threatening at a particular time.

This book can also be helpful after you have finished treatment. You may find that it takes time to feel physically and emotionally at home in the world again and to make sense out of what you've been through.

In the back of the book there are three appendices: quick and easy breathing exercises helpful for times of high anxiety or limited mobility; a list of some national American and Canadian cancer organizations that provide a wide array of information and support, followed by thoughts about how to assess support groups; and some other practical and emotional support resources: a few tapes and books, and an organization where you can get information about Focusing, and a guide to chemotherapy.

About Me and My Healing Biases

My approaches to healing spring from my personal history and my particular personality strengths and vulnerabilities.

At age forty, middle age set in with a bang, changing my life abruptly and painfully. I left a long happy, suddenly war-torn workplace and, with it, fifteen years of teaching. I was lured back to writing fiction, which I'd abandoned in my twenties. Over the next four years, both my parents and my two pairs of aunts and uncles died. Six months later, I developed painful menstrual problems that were unresponsive to long-term medical treatment accompanied by imagery and psychological work. I ultimately required a hysterectomy. I also had recurrent pain and immobility from a herniated disc and muscle spasms.

To deal with all this and the enormous transition from working with people out in the world to working alone at home, I started down the path of the psyche. I learned self-hypnosis and an emotional processing technique called Focusing, kept a journal, and entered into deep and extensive psychotherapy with Jungian aspects. For all my difficulties, I also felt a tremendous excitement of adventure, self-discovery, and development of new skills and interests. And throughout the ups and downs I was gradually becoming a writer.

At forty-eight, my first breast cancer was found; a second, unrelated one at fifty-two. Both were detected early by routine mammograms. The first was the "least" of breast cancers, requiring only a lumpectomy and radiation, and had an excellent prognosis. The second was a nasty, fast-growing, highly atypical cancer that had spread to lymph nodes and required very aggressive treatment. As this book goes to press, I am fifty-six years old and have been cancer-free for almost four years.

The prevalent views that we participate in the onset of our disease, and that we can cure or heal ourselves through certain mental, psychological, or spiritual practices, self-change, or change in diet and lifestyle have an upside and a downside—whether we believe all or only certain parts of them. If they give us a sense of empowerment, they are positive. They can set us on a path of exploration and change which engenders hope and actions to take, and unleash emotional and physiological healing mechanisms. They can also help restore a sense of control that disease undermines, and may give us significant emotional and spiritual healing, whatever our physical outcome. The downside prevails if these views provoke self-blame, a sense of failure, or pressure, when we are already under duress, to work even harder or in some incompatible way.

Precisely because of my background in psychological work, my belief in the healing value of inner change, and my awareness of the connections between mind and body, I cannot dismiss such views with a wave of the hand, and yet they are threatening to me. They tend to activate my over-responsibility and my anxious inner critic. In short, they get me in my vulnerabilities.

For both cancers, I felt I had positive ways to support myself through treatment and could bring a lot to aid my own healing. But I also felt that I had burdened myself with too heavy a responsibility for healing the menstrual disorder and had had to grapple with feelings of failure, and I did not want to do that again.

Regarding the theory of emotional or lifestyle causes of cancer, I knew instinctively with the first cancer that such a view could only add distress, so I kept away from it. That I had to encounter the issue with the second cancer was inevitable, and you will see me skirmish with it in a couple of the original letters. My feeling then and now is that when engaged in the task of healing, I do better not to focus on the causes of my cancers, which could equally include other things largely out of my control. The earlier pile up of stressful events, not having had or breast-fed babies, years of eating the Great American Diet—though I was a low-fat/high-fiber vegetarian by the time of the second cancer—a tendency to overweight, and who knows what combination of environmental carcinogens, genes, or other culprits yet to be discovered by further much-needed research are all possible causes for a disease that has become epidemic.

So regardless of whether these theories are true, it is not helpful or healing for me to think that way. And the bottom line is I look for whatever helps toward healing. For me, that means both going down to my innermost center and connecting to others. It means using skills I enjoy and being lured by whatever gives me a sense of magic and adventure. It also means I need to watch out that I don't feel pressured to take on some program for healing, for my strengths are in spontaneity and creativity. The medical program is already demanding enough! For you, it may be something different—following a clearly laid-out program, some one meaningful practice, a variety of healing and pleasurable activities, entering psychotherapy to explore emotional logjams, altering your diet or work load, going to a support group, or simply taking good care of yourself. You may already have a sense of what will serve you best or you may determine it as you go along.

There is no single truth or healing method that is right for everyone. I believe some kind of participation can enhance healing and may make all the difference. I believe that self-love and a degree of trust in our own powers can play an important role. I don't think the experts, no matter how many patients they've studied, know all the answers. But I do think each person—whether "expert," doctor, nurse, psychologist, or patient— adds something to our understanding. We are all explorers. We all add our bit, and whatever your bit is, it's probably your best healing path.

October 4

Dear Friends,

Bad news. Breast cancer again. Four years later. This time in my other breast. Picked up on annual mammogram. Sorry not to write individually and more personally, but I need to make contact and this is the way I can best do it right now.

This is a more serious situation not only because of recurrence, but because of the nature of the new stuff that showed on the mammogram. It was multiple, widely spread somethings, not familiar or evidently malignant to the long-experienced radiologist. So, from the beginning a mastectomy loomed as a likely possibility if it proved to be cancer.

Because my surgeon was away, I had some time for good old Judy emotional processing, which has been beneficial in dealing with all the feelings, imaginings, and possibilities that have come up. On my doctor's return, he outlined a series of information-gathering steps. I immediately had a needle biopsy of one of the places, which surprised everyone by coming back malignant. So I am now recovering from a surgical biopsy with general anesthesia which will tell us whether other stuff is also malignant. We are in the process of learning the extent of this and heading toward powwows, second opinions, and decisions about treatment.

In addition to the fear of cancer itself, this feels like a terrible setback, because during the last couple of months I was writing like an angel, on a glorious, productive roll on my book about the first cancer and my use of inner techniques for healing and self-support. I had just commented that the chapter I was working on lacked dramatic focus. Well, it's got it now: "We interrupt this program with an emergency news bulletin: Cancer again!" But, hey, come on, Universe, I'm a good enough writer that I could have dealt with a need for dramatic focus purely as a technical problem!

In the now almost three weeks since the mammogram, I've felt and explored so much: shock, fear, anger, and mule heel-digging-in resistance.

I've also realized that I have all the resources I had the last time, some of them even more developed. I have been astonished at my own ability to be with whatever comes up for me and then feel it shift. This is particularly due to my engagement over the last couple of years with the inner processing technique of Focusing. Even a body-overwhelming terror that hit one morning, when received and worked with "in a Focusing way," shifted in about an hour, leaving me feeling my tremendous, humble powers and trust in myself to meet this crisis.

I also know that every one of the tough events of my middle age has given me wonderful learnings and personal development. (However, at the moment I'm not so fond of the word *growth* as I have been!) Whatever I learn and whatever I am able to do that is new becomes part of me and is mine to keep long after the difficulty has passed.

I know how to hunker down and look after myself and I know my ability to have adventure and to experience life intensely and meaningfully along the way. I have already received many gifts from inside and outside.

John is deep in this, too. For richer, for poorer, in sickness and in health, he's been getting more than his share of being the suppporting other. But along with the stress, a lot of good stuff is going on between us.

Other people, too, are among my resources. Cancer has meanings that everyone grapples with—so I understand if contact is difficult for you. But if you're comfortable being in touch with me through the coming process of treatments, you will add to my healing power.

You need have no fears of intrusion. Mail can be opened when wanted and the telephone has an answering machine. I will put updates on the machine, so you can be informed even if other things keep me from talking to you. But even if you don't hear from me, you can be sure I will receive fully all gifts of friendship and add them to my healing resources.

Love, Judy

Dear Reader—Cancer Patient, Cancer Veteran,
                    and Grappler with other Frays and Frazzles of Life,

In these letters, which alternate with the original ones to my friends, I
will be here for you as I was present and loving for myself during treatment. Perhaps you feel overwhelmed by whatever is upon you, or perhaps
you have weathered the worst of the storm and now need to make sense
of it and put your pieces back together in a fresh and life-giving way.

I hope these offerings will help you discover and celebrate your own
best resources and style, adapting whichever of mine work for you. Perhaps you will develop new coping skills. It's often hard to see while you're
in the thick, but sooner or later you are bound to take your own measure
and be astonished by your "copability." That's my word that says a lot
about us in tough times. I bet it applies to you. You may want to remind
yourself from time to time that no matter how bumpy the ride, *you are
coping*.

Because writing is a natural resource for me, many of my suggestions are geared toward writing. But just reading them or playing around in
your head with them may help you. You may want to try out other forms,
such as drawing, painting, sounds, movement, or any combination that
works for you. An advantage of writing is that it gives you something

concrete to do, something tangible to look back on which, over time, becomes a record of development.

So, my first suggestion is that you make a list of your natural resources or skills you already have. I think you'll find that some of them can be applied or adapted to help you cope with what's happening to you. (If you're waiting in line or at a doctor's office or lying in bed, you can play with this in your head.) Make it like a grocery list or embroider and explore in detail whichever things draw you to do so.

For instance, I am outgoing and like to relate to people. I take this for granted in ordinary life. During cancer treatment, I realized that this natural behavior was one of my best anxiety busters. I could exchange a moment of conversation or laughter with secretaries, nurses, doctors, technicians, housecleaners, hospital volunteers, parking lot attendants, or other patients and gain a sense of connectedness.

Perhaps you are scientifically or technologically inclined and will find a measure of control by learning about the latest findings on breast cancer, procedures, and hi-tech hardware. Perhaps you like clothes or interior decorating and can while away waiting room time by mentally redesigning the space or re-outfitting people around you. Perhaps you have a religion or a spiritual practice that is sustaining. Maybe you're good at making up limericks about whatever is going on or do impromptu impersonations. Or you know how to make lists and delegate responsibilities in the household to meet needs changed by your new situation.

Does my lack of hierarchy jar you or provoke laughter? Whatever higgledy piggledy ideas emerge are valid. Both the ability to "redecorate" and a spiritual practice have their place in healing and may serve you well at different moments during this difficult time. And as the world you've been pitched into can feel like a crazy juxtaposition of motley neighbors, the idiosyncracy of your own bag of tricks is a grand way to meet it.

Perhaps you want to consider what kinds of practical resources you have at your disposal or how inventive you are already becoming. Before going into surgery, I signed up for a home-delivery video rental so that I would have easy access to entertainment when I couldn't get out. What friends might you call on for what purposes? People want to help, and often letting them know what you need gives them a way to do it. Some are better at offering concrete help—delivering a meal, picking up a prescription, or taking you to an appointment; others are good listeners when you need to talk.

If you feel you don't have many resources to write down, you might revisit this practice from time to time and make additions. Perhaps you'll gradually identify things you now take for granted or see new skills developing. Or maybe just reading this will set a process in motion, and over the next few days ideas will pop into your mind.

Sometimes it's helpful to recall times in your life when you were up against difficulties and identify ways you handled them. Sometimes when I do this I feel the strength of my coping abilities, but at other moments I feel anguished and think, None of that was as big and difficult and threatening as this. Then I remember that I didn't "know how" to meet those situations either, and that I don't have to "know how" now. A more knowing, less conscious part of me knows quite a lot, and I identify the "how" only as I see it unfold or as I look back at what I have just done.

You might want to create a sentence or two to say in your mind at those moments when you are hit by the terror that you can't cope or won't be able to cope in the future.

Something like:

"I don't have to know how."
*

"I have everything within me that I need for this."
*

"Some part of me knows whatever I need to know."
*

"A knowing, able part of me is guiding (will guide) me."
*

Here's to you and your not-knowing-how know-how.

Love, Judy

October 28

Dear Friends,

First, incredible thanks for your outpouring of love: phone calls, flowers, letters, balloons, packages, visits, food. Perhaps the most unusual has been a barber shop quartet on my answering machine! I feel your presence, and, believe me, it makes all the difference.

Second, the medical picture. For those of you who haven't heard from John, me, or the answering machine about the pathology reports, I'm sorry to say they're worse than expected. The surgical biopsy showed "any number more" malignant nodes in the breast. Because of my cancer history and risk of recurrence, because of my back problems which would be aggravated by lopsidedness, and because of difficulty matching a breast as large as mine if I opt to have reconstruction surgery, the surgeon recommended double mastectomy with removal of lymph nodes on the right side. (Left side nodes went last time.) Ten out of ten lymph nodes removed were affected and surely so are others.

The nature of the cancer cells is not nice. Apparently there are cancer cells that more resemble breast cells, and that's the better situation, and cancer cells that are more dissimilar, which is worse. Mine are the latter. It's less predictable how they'll respond to treatment, though I've been told it's often these fast-growing cells that get most effectively zapped by chemotherapy and radiation. This is not a recurrence of the prior cancer. It is a second primary cancer. The breast treated last time is healthy. On the one hand, it's good that it's not a recurrence. On the other, this is a much nastier cancer than the first.

My doctors are shocked by the pathology reports, too. They are taking my case to the Tumor Board, where doctors present cases and pick each other's brains. The good part is the doctors I have on the team: all get an A+ for medical abilities, personalities, and communication skills. Two other important pluses are negative bone and liver scans done the week before surgery. Probably both chemotherapy and radiation will be used, but the actual plan will be constructed when we meet with the oncologist on November 2. Treatment will begin three to four weeks after surgery to allow appropriate healing time.

This is shocking news for you to absorb, too. I want you to know, at least, that there is no particular way you have to be for me. I am not afraid of your feelings or mine. To the extent possible and comfortable for you, a broad base of caring friends for us—please don't forget John and his need for contact and respite—can greatly add to my healing powers.

*　　*　　*

And now, the tale.

The last week before surgery is a gallop of medical dates: bone scan, liver scan, oncologist, second-opinion surgeon, my surgeon for post-biopsy checkup. Icing on the cake: a respiratory infection for which I have to see yet another doctor—my internist is on vacation—in hopes of clearing it up in time for surgery.

More icing on the cake: car in shop for three days of those appointments to the tune of almost $700. The mechanics are noble in my behalf, but there is tense stuff about payment. The head mechanic finally gets the money man to agree to let me postdate my check twenty-four hours while monies are transferred. When we go to pick up the car, they can't find the paperwork, but we are allowed to take the car without paying. I find notes for the paperwork on the car floor and John trundles them back.

The day before surgery the repair place is still confused: the secretary on other end of line, flipping through papers: "Are you Mr. North?"

John: "How much is Mr. North's bill?"

"$87."

John: "Yes, indeed, then. I'm Mr. North."

From the other end of the line, tentatively: "You are?"

The hospital calls the same day, less than twenty-four hours before surgery, requesting we bring my 20% of $6,000 with us to the hospital. John fantasizes identifying himself on any further money telephone calls as Mr. Turnip, Mr. Stone, or Mr. Chapter 11 Bankruptcy. ("I'm sorry, sir, we don't have any of those names in our computer.")

With all this finally behind us, the medical insurance forms sent in, and a system set up to deal with incoming bills, I go to the park to let my stress flow out while walking in nature. After a half mile, pleased that waning respiratory infection permits this gentle exercise, I turn back.

Suddenly I can't keep my balance. Holy cow! I didn't realize how bad my stress was! Am I having a stroke? A heart attack? An inner ear disturbance? I walk carefully and everything seems to be okay, but my anxiety is not alleviated.

As I drive out of the park, I see a huge smoke plume rising from downtown Berkeley. Criminy, everything's going whacko. On the spur of the moment, I stop at a friend's en route home, for a last pre-surgery hug. People are gathered in her normally quiet street and someone is positioning a loud radio on the sill of an upstairs window.

"Where were you?" my friend asks with such uncharacteristic intensity that I think, How can she be mad I'm late when she didn't know I was coming? That's when I learn there's been an earthquake.

"Thank God! The problem isn't in my body!" I exclaim and feel my anxiety melt. Then I take in what I've been told: It's a big earthquake and the Bay Bridge has collapsed. I've been living so completely with the unreality of my own earthquake for the past five weeks since the mammogram that the only thoughts that break through my spaciness are: Is John okay? The house? Will surgery happen? I drive home feeling everything is up for grabs.

John and the house are fine. I have a rush of gratitude that I am alive. Something bigger has displaced my cancer. We sock in with TV. The proof that disaster is real is that all channels are covering it, there are no ads, and anchor Wendy Tokuda's hair is being visibly blown by fans distributed in the studio to help cool the special generators, because the power is out. At 11:00, we switch off the television, losing the welcome absorption in a different disaster. I return to my own reality and pack my suitcase.

*   *   *

We're at the hospital at 7 a.m. We surgery patients form a little club. One woman hoped the earthquake would postpone her surgery. Not me. I've been on hold too long already. I need to move along.

I come through the surgery well. I am blessed with a wonderful hospital roommate and some pretty fine nurses. One seems familiar and I ask if she lives in a certain town a little distance away.

"Yes," she replies. Before she can form the obvious question, I continue.

"And did you, four years ago, get stopped by a cop at a brand new stop sign you didn't see, and when he looked at your licence and saw the photo of you with your eyes closed, say, 'Since the State of California has seen fit to licence you to drive with your eyes closed, I can hardly give you a ticket for not seeing that stop sign'?"

Her astonishment confirms my hunch. I tell her I had her as a nurse during my last cancer.

        *   *   *

      Two days after surgery I receive a visit from a special cancer nurse, who talks to me about many practical and emotional issues and about resources available to me. We have been engrossed for a half hour when my surgeon arrives in his operating room greens. The clinical nurse moves discreetly to the end of the bed. As my surgeon slowly gives out the pathology news, heaping one unsavory piece upon another, the nurse glides up on the other side of the bed, takes my hand and holds and strokes it. The stripes on the privacy curtain start to wobble and do the be-bop, and I say, "I think I'm in shock." Both of them nod and now my doctor takes my other hand. As I lie there sinking deep into the bed supported by those caring hands, I think, How is it possible to go to battle as I will need to go to battle? I couldn't even get out of this bed. Then instantly I know that all I need to do is be here in this moment, and mentally I put an arm around the Judy who is in shock. When my doctor finishes, I say in a quiet voice, "I'm sorry." He jars and says, "You stole my lines. That's what I was going to say."

      "That's okay," I answer. "It's okay for both of us to be sorry." My "I'm sorry" sounds as if it were directed to my surgeon, and a small part of it is, because I know he cares for me and that telling a patient bad news is always hard. But the major part of my "I'm sorry" is directed to myself, to the Judy who is rocked by the doctor's report. Already I am offering myself a shorthand expression of loving support.

After the doctor departs, the nurse stays on, an extraordinary supportive presence. John comes in and I have to hit him with the bad news. The nurse stays for us both, then at exactly the right moment, she leaves us to ourselves. John and I continue to let in the news and visit until he leaves to seek the familiarity of the house and get some much-needed sleep.

A couple of hours later, I feel my body shift and lighten and my spirits change. The shock is wearing off. Oh, wonders of the body and the psyche. Pretty soon I am making my first unescorted perambulations to the bathroom and hall, my body progressing on its healing course. The licenced-to-drive-with-eyes-closed afternoon nurse comes on duty, and she, my roommate, and I engage in pleasant, humorous interaction.

*   *   *

The next morning I wake from a dream that I am walking along corridors to meet someone in an airport. Beside me at a little distance walks another woman, a silent supportive part of myself. Wearing my hospital gown and bandage across my chest, I finally come to the end where I am to meet the arriving traveler.

There, filling one third of the area, a whole battalion of fresh young soldiers is gathering into marching formation.

A couple of weeks ago, I noted in my journal how different I felt this time than the first time I had cancer. Then, images of guns and war bored me. I didn't need them and my imagination went to polar bears and Tweedledum and Tweedledee. "But this time," I wrote, " *This is war!*"

Thank you, dear psyche.

Thank you for sending me my troops.

Love, Judy

Dear Reader,

A lot of readers of my letters have asked me about Focusing, because it was one of the cornerstones of my self-support. It is beyond the scope of this book to give you directions for Focusing, and though not impossible, few people learn the skill from a book alone. In the appendix, I tell you where to locate Focusing resources, including trainers nationwide and internationally. What I want to offer you in this letter is a journal entry I did when seized by panic soon after I learned that I had cancer. It illustrates several elements of Focusing that may be helpful to you without any training.

*   *   *

6:30 a.m. Friday, Sept. 29

I'm being hit by a full-blown attack of terror and panic and I've been trying to think what I can do for myself. The first thing is to receive this terror here, not run away from it, not try to change it. All I'm looking for is to invite this frantic terror to come and sit with me. As I make that invitation, I realize I already have an image of it racing back and forth on a deck in front of me. I'm in a seaside house with a big expanse of picture window to the sea, but this panic is tearing back and forth on the weathered gray deck, kind of crazed out there, blocking my view.

Hmm . . . I feel a little easing. Because it's out there, it's no longer occupying my whole body. Now I want to invite it again to come and sit beside me. I want us first just to see the pots of geraniums along the low rail and the sand and the ocean beyond. Yeah, already without that tearing back and forth, things feel a little better.

This tearing back and forth is a product of my mind and it's the global fears about this thing bursting in on my life, irrevocably shooting to hell all I've established. I need to remember how I felt before this happened—the satisfaction of the balanced rhythms of living and writing that I'd established.

Just now I stopped writing and allowed my tears to flow, tears of sadness, loss, inexorableness. All I've built hasn't been enough to prevent this from happening. It's as if whatever unresolved in my life has escalated its physical attacks on my body. I would have thought I had been healing so extensively that I wouldn't get such a major physical hit. Getting this cancer makes me feel as if something keeps running after me and overtaking me. No wonder I feel panicked. No wonder that panic has been racing around. I couldn't prevent this. I just glanced at one of Ashleigh Brilliant's Potshot signs I bought last week: "I try to take one day at a time, but sometimes several days attack at once." I intended mentally to revise it with "my whole life attacks at once." Instead what came out was "several lives attack at once."

So this is the root of the terror: that my whole life—or my life and the intertwining, generational lives of my family—are all attacking at once. No wonder my terror is so great, greater than whatever I have to deal with here now. I don't know what all that consists of yet, but it's not an invalidation of me and my life. Oh, so that's it: I've been feeling as if getting cancer again is an invalidation of me, my process, my changing, my learning—a lot of pretty basic values—as well as tearing into the thing I've spent the last twelve years working to develop: my writing. Okay. No wonder I've been panicked! A big letting go there.

Now I can separate some things. Of course it's not a statement about me and my choices. And I don't know yet who I will become out of this. I don't know yet what this piece will provide. I can also separate the value of where I had come to before this happened from the pain of having it taken away—or interrupted. The cancer has taken away only this phase. The quality of the phase and its achievements remain valid. What I've been working on remains valid. I remain valid.

I can feel more letting go now, another little shift in my body as I just take time to stay fully with this new awareness. At the root of this terror then was a sweeping invalidation of me, my goals, my choices. And here's another piece: fear that this will tear me apart, undermine, or rip my personality. Just saying that helps.

Suddenly now comes "the little engine that could," and I know I will take this the same way as other difficult times—a piece at a time. A part of me is still unready, unwilling to give up this extraordinary time I have been living in and accept what I'm going into, and that is very understandable. I worked hard to come into a place of harmony. I moved through the fear of taking on such a big project. I have ridden my work well. I stand in a new relationship to the writer in me and to the work I am creating. The knowledge of that is very important to affirm.

How are you now, my terror? I reach my hand out to you. You seem to have put your feet up on the railing, and together we can stare out over the sand to the sea and wonder about something that is larger and more spiritual than what I have felt negatively engulfing me. We will cope as we are already coping because we don't have to encompass everything at once—just whatever is going on now. And we can feel the love we have for ourselves and others and the love others have for us.

*   *   *

As you can see, a great deal of change took place in my feelings in the process of that writing: I moved from panic to a calm, spirtual place. Here are some features of Focusing imbedded in that journal piece.

Focusing assumes that our emotional experience is made up of more than that which we are fully aware of, even if we have a name like "panic" or "terror" for it. In Focusing we attend our bodily sense of the subtle mix of feelings and meanings and small bodily shifts that accompany further understanding and change.

The most fundamental attitude of Focusing is to approach whatever is inside with friendly curiosity and to follow whatever is happening there. Friendly curiosity sounds awfully calm for this upheaval! Nonetheless, my second and third sentences establish my invitation to accept and be with my feelings: "The first thing is to receive this terror here, not run away from it, not try to change it. All I'm looking for is to invite this frantic terror to come and sit with me."

Next, I found the right distance from what was threatening to overwhelm me, so that I could still stay in relationship to it. By inviting my panic to sit with me, I put it outside me yet still close by. It established me as more than and a little separate from it, already partly an observer. This can be tremendously helpful in difficult situations.

There are a number of images that you can try when you feel overwhelmed. You can put the whole bundle of feelings and meanings in your lap, on your knee, across the room, or any other place that allows you to feel less engulfed. (I once had to place something all the way across the San Francisco Bay!) Or, rather than putting "it" out, you can imagine moving yourself to a comfortable spot, as I did once when I imagined going up to a high place from which I could look down at what was going on. If you feel shaky, in a vortex, or an eddy, you can place yourself on solid ground a little distance away. The important thing is not to abandon what you've moved away from or placed outside. Sometimes it doesn't want to move out and may respond well to being allowed to stay and be heard and comforted. Then you may imagine putting an arm around it, making more space inside yourself around it, or breathing around it. This is not an arbitrary process. The body knows when you've got it right, and you will feel a slight shift or easing when you find the appropriate distance.

The spontaneous image of my panic racing outside on a deck constituted the next step of Focusing: letting a word or image emerge. By describing how your inner experience feels, you become its observer, rather than its victim. Again, this is not arbitrary. When you listen inside your body, it will tell you when you've got it just right. The skills of Focusing are in learning to listen inside and check back with the body to see if the words are right. I knew I had it right, because things were easing inside me.

Next, I stopped writing and just gave myself time to be with what was happening, in this case intense feelings of loss.

Then came new learning about the panic. It wasn't about the fear of cancer itself, but the fact that at that moment I experienced the resurgence of cancer as being overrun by my personal history, in spite of all the inner work I'd done. When I became aware of that new information, I said, "No wonder." Think how it feels when you are upset about something and someone gives you an understanding response. "No wonder" or some other expression of compassionate understanding can do a lot inside when you have just grasped why something is painful, hard, or infuriating. My acknowledgment was so powerful that the core of the panic revealed itself: I felt invalidated in fundamental life choices and personal meanings. Once I had that, I could also distinguish the feeling from the reality. It is a remarkable beauty of the psyche how quickly a shift can take place when we have gotten the full story. Note that I didn't do anything to change my panic. Once I grasped what it was made up of, a huge shift took place, and "the little engine that could" appeared.

This writing illustrates a frequent and lovely result of a Focusing session: the discovery of unexpected, underlying meanings and spontaneous shifts in both meaning and feeling. You don't get such large shifts every time, but even small shifts can make a significant difference.

Next time you are scared or overwhelmed, feel free to try out any of these activities. If something seems too big, consider seeking the right distance. This can be a helpful prelude to making a difficult decision, medical or otherwise.

Is there is any part of you that would appreciate your willingness to receive it in a friendly way or feel comforted by your putting an arm around it? You might try coming up with other images of receiving and comforting that would be just right for you. And if something is unclear, see if a word or image might come if you invite (but do not force) it. Just contemplating a word or image can often decrease the sense of chaos.

I hope my writing about my panic will assure you that you are not alone. Your feelings and personal meanings will differ from mine, but if you receive them kindly, whether they do or don't make sense, your body and psyche may surprise you with unexpected gifts.

Love, Judy

November 27

Dear Friends,

More thanks. More hugs. More tale.

I return from the hospital Saturday, October 21. Three days later I have my first appointment with my surgeon, who removes the bandage and inspects his handiwork while having me avert my gaze by counting cobwebs on the ceiling. There aren't any. I should have brought my house along. He removes staples and one drainage bag. When I get off the table and see a few staples that he missed sweeping into the trash, I think, Good grief, when he said staples, he meant staples—office variety.

When I get home, I have a headache and am shaky from the trip. As I grope in the medicine chest for some pain reliever, bottles hurl themselves like lemmings into the buckets of water below—because of the drought, we're still water savers—and suddenly I feel panicked and overwhelmed. John comes in to rescue the plunging bottles while I retreat to receive my tears and sobs, the first to come since the pathology report. I had expected them earlier, but I seem to be working on maximum efficiency. When I first got home from the hospital, I was busy adapting and providing for basic physical needs. Now as I let my whole body express my loss and fear, I feel release, along with pride in my savvy psyche. I don't need to worry that I'm blocking emotions. I can trust my psyche's timing and ability to serve all my needs.

When I quiet, I put words to my feeling: "Yeah, that was a real panic attack." I ask John to sit with me for a little bit while I talk and gradually contact the origin of my intense feelings.

The appointment with my surgeon gave me three major belts of awareness. While waiting in the examining room, I thought about how the last time I'd seen my doctor in this room, I was a healthy four-year lumpectomy veteran, and now here I was with a double mastectomy. Then, when he removed the bandage for the first time, I felt my vulnerability. And when he touched the area, I felt my flatness.

*   *   *

Soon I am drafting a letter to friends, my first activity that connects me to writing and to people without their being present on the phone or in person. My resources expand and John regains pieces of his life. He is best man at a friend's wedding. Meals On Wheels will never match the dinner that comes home for me from that wedding reception!

On another visit to the surgeon, I stop to say howdy at my internist's office, which is on the ground floor of the same building. He is just back from vacationing in France. Normally he hugs me, but today he gives me a kiss on each cheek, French style. "Hey," I say, "your trip to France really left its effect on you."

"I look forward to your being able to receive hugs again as a sign of your healing," he answers.

With my hand now on the open waiting room door, I turn back and say, "Thanks for the French kisses." My words cause us both a good jolt. My brain goes into high gear; simultaneously I struggle to straighten out my language problems, imagining the lurid headline, "Doctor in Jail on Ethical Charges," and frantically scan the waiting room, hoping the elderly Asian lady doesn't speak English and the septuagenarian gent is deaf.

*   *   *

On October 31, I have two events: at the end of the day, the pleasurable visits of neighborhood ghosts and goblins for candy; in the morning, the last visit to my surgeon before my "unveiling." Everything is healing on schedule. I am given the green light to exercise my lymph node arm, and now it's up to me to view my changed chest in my own home, in my own time, in my own way. So far, I am not ready to look under the ace bandage and gauze that have been given me for purely psychological protection.

After the goblins and space characters have gone back to their home planets, I talk to John about my fears. Then in the peaceful dark of night, I write in my journal:

I love you, Judy, and whatever my chest looks like, I am still Judy. I am afraid that I'll be emotionally overwhelmed or/and squeamish. It is okay to have and fully receive whatever feelings come up.

I want to suggest here that my psyche will be able to modulate what comes in, and that however intense my feelings, they will not overwhelm me, because I can be with them "in a Focusing way." That means that as a first step I can "set a feeling out on my knee" or even farther away if I need to. I can handle things by increments.

I'd like to suggest to my unconscious that tonight, during sleep, we do the work to help prepare me to feel ready and challenged:

I will receive the body that is new to me.

I will receive my feelings.

I will comfort and hold myself as needed.

I will accompany myself on this voyage into the unknown.

I will enjoy the development of self that comes out this.

I will remember the life-saving reasons for this.

I will fantasize appreciating my freedom from the burden of large breasts as a benefit to my back.

I will imagine myself entering a new realm.

I will honor all that I am.

I will honor adaptability.

I will honor the unexpected journey of life.

I will honor what is larger than my vision and my understanding.

I will swim across this river that divides my former body shape and my new body contour and surface.

I am Judy, the traveler of the psyche.

I will continue my journey.

*   *   *

I sleep well and wake refreshed. John and I are both ready to take our first look—at just one small area. As soon as we have looked, our anxieties melt. I am bathed in relief and know I can do the rest a little at a time.

A couple of hours later, a friend takes me to my first non-medical appointment, a haircut, and afterward we go to buy camisoles. Trying them on causes the ace bandage to gape and the gauze to emerge. With each tug, another portion of my chest is revealed. By the time I have selected the camisoles I want, I have seen every part of my chest, though not all at once. By that night, bandage and gauze moving at odds are driving me nuts. I pull a new camisole over them and remove the bulky swaddling from underneath. By the next day I am ready to see my body "steadily and see it whole."

The trick was in giving myself permission to do the job gradually. At the same time, I knew this afternoon's first meeting with the oncologist would start me into the next phase—the nitty gritty of plans for chemo-therapy—and I was aware I didn't want to face two big things at once. I have come in just under the wire to present myself for the next step.

*   *   *

John accompanies me to the oncologist. Being a non-scientist in Oncology 101, I appreciate having as many brains, ears, and notetakers as

37

possible. We decide this time we don't need a tape recorder. Oh, foolish we!

The doctor asks how I'm doing, recovering from surgery.

"Pretty well, thanks. Doing nicely."

Then, whap! Two more wet socks in the face. Sock #1: my estrogen receptors are negative, which is not good and eliminates one of the less-toxic treatment options. Sock #2: I came in expecting to talk about chemotherapy and now a whole new idea is introduced. The doctor would like to "harvest" bone marrow to be kept frozen in case a pretty drastic, but potentially life-saving, treatment is needed down the line.

I feel myself go into shock again. John gently removes the yellow pad and immobilized pencil from my lap and takes charge. The rest of the appointment is a swirl of clearly stated information with brief review lessons which I try to restate, but finally give up on. The names of the chemotherapy drugs make Welsh look like an easy language. I am shown a picture of a "portacath," a metal broachlike gadget with a cushion center, which will be surgically implanted in my chest to receive and distribute the chemo. The slick brochure photograph shimmers in front of me and if there is further explanation about the portacath, it passes me by. I've learned not to worry when this happens. I take in what I can and know there will be other opportunities to hear the information again.

How come I don't want to kill the messenger? Because he is calm, clear, and highly responsive. The minute he sees by my body language that a question is forming, he stops, listens, and then replies. This is a

mixed blessing because shock is causing my mouth to do a perfect imper-
sonation of a fish, while this patient doctor is still acting as if there is a
human brain on call in my upper chambers. He says the first thing we
should do is make appointments for a heart scan—"to see if your heart is
okay"—and a bone marrow biopsy.

"Hey," I say, regaining my verbal skills, "my heart was just fine
before I came in here today."

He picks up the phone to make the first appointment and repeats
the time the secretary suggests: 8 a.m., Tuesday. I marvel that he has the
same reaction as I to the preposterousness of the hour and adjusts it to
11. When I mention this to John later, he tells me that when I heard the
appointment time, I staged an instant total body collapse response, complete with eyes rolled up toward the ceiling, which this humanitarian doctor
correctly translated and acted upon.

It is now about 5:30, and as we drive in the dusk, John asks what I
want to do about supper.

"Be served," is my succinct response. We drive to our favorite pizza
place, and while waiting for takeout, we walk up and down the street. An
exquisite new moon with Venus nestled at its chin is etched against the
darkening blue-black sky, people are settling down to eat pizza, and next
door, others are browsing in a bookstore. Ordinary life hums around me
and beauty hangs aloft, and my life, as I know it, is being snatched away
from me. My arm linked to John's for physical as well as emotional sup-

port, a few tears trickling down my cheek, I lean on his shoulder and say several times, "I don't understand."

I listen for what I mean by that. It's not the issue of "How unfair." Nor is it "What caused this?" It's more a feeling of being hurled onto an alien planet, where the entire culture is different, and the mind is desperately trying to make sense of the unfamiliar. Also floating through is a vague feeling that somewhere along the line I must have made a poor decision to land in such a mess, like a drunk who put all his life savings on one number in Reno and can't even remember having done it.

Pesto pizza and talk at our familiar kitchen table are every bit as effective for shock as brandy. I recover enough to go to the regular Focusing group that night. I am warmly greeted and discover that my chest and arm can now receive full hugs. People tell me that it is far better to see and hear me, even in this peak of crisis, than if I hadn't come. I cannot protect them, but they, like me, have confidence in the ability to process their feelings.

*   *   *

A few days later, someone asks if I am doing physical therapy to help extend the range of motion in the arm that had the lymph nodes removed. John says, "You bet she is. I put the remains of the Halloween candy on the top shelf of the pantry."

I greet my chiropractor with both arms extended high above my head. "Go ahead, guess, which arm had the lymph node surgery?" Only her surgeon knows for sure.

*   *   *

A close friend says she wants to tell me something she hopes won't upset me. I invite her to go ahead.

"I was feeling awful recently and asked myself what it was about," she says. "I discovered it was about you and asked myself what was the worst of it. The worst is a fear that you might die. The next worst is that even if you're going to be okay, you have to go through such a long rough spell. I feel bad for you and I feel bad that it will interfere with the kind of time we normally have together. And isn't it awful that I should be so selfish to think of that when you have to deal with cancer? And now as I speak to you, I hope it isn't horrible for you to hear these things."

"On the contrary," I answer. "Your telling me makes me feel fully connected to you, and of course I've thought of all these things from my own perspective. It touches me to be told that what I contribute to your life is important and it's hard to have it taken away. If you continue to share your real feelings, we won't lose our access to each other any more than the demands of treatment require. And, in case you have any doubts, I'm going to do everything in my power and use every resource in my reach to live as long and healthily as I can."

We talk on, having exactly the kind of visit that is part of our ordinary lives. Later, I tell this story to another close friend who has been trying to spare me by not telling me how my cancer is affecting her. It opens up the passage between us again. As I share the story with others, I hear their relief. Another friend tells me that one of her fears is that she won't be a good enough friend to me. My own fears include my inability to be as involved in others' lives as I usually am. Mentally, physically, and emotionally, my attention is requisitioned at the moment.

*   *   *

John takes me to a wig salon recommended by a friend who is a chemotherapy veteran. We enter a world of slender styrofoam heads topped by coiffs ordinary and coiffs far-out. But the central attraction is a fellow customer, a large, amiable blonde, who bustles in and out carting wigs she needs to have "done."

This lady is "into" wigs the way I collect rubber stamps. She owns a hundred and is now bringing in the ten or twelve she will take with her to Hawaii on vacation.

"Looking after them is no trouble at all," she proselytizes enthusiastically. "Why, really, they take less time than doing your hair and makeup."

No feature has been left as nature drew it on this ample face. Eyebrows, lashes, mouth have all been lovingly reconstructed and all surfaces repaved. I take in her outfit: dramatic diagonals, an enormous magenta ceramic jungle feline on a curved prowl of her neckline, stiletto-heeled

42

shoes with open-toed, see-through plastic tops. I dub her "Las Vegas Lil."

What a dullard I am, limiting myself to matching my hairstyle and color. Wild Judy thinks: Forget the graying brown wig! I'll take one punk purple, one blonde bouffant, and one frosted number with locks that meet under the chin. And do you have a catalog? My rubber stamp companies all have catalogs.

*   *   *

The shape of the next week changes radically three times. Will there or won't there be time to fit in non-medical but closely related priorities? I want to do my own work to help the chemotherapy be as effective as possible. So in addition to the heart scan and bone marrow biopsy, I am getting recommendations and going to appointments to try out several healer/hypnotherapy/visualization-imagery people.

I return from one of these appointments to find John perplexed. The office of a doctor he has never heard of has called and set up an appointment for surgery for the coming Tuesday.

"Oh, that has to be Dr. Vascular," I tell John, "the one who will implant the portacath. A number of possible names were run by me in my drug haze at the bone marrow biopsy, and this must be the man selected. They've scheduled surgery sooner than the date they told me, and now it and pre-op testing and appointments to meet both surgeons—Dr. Vascular and Dr. Bone Marrow—are overlapping with the psyche appointments I made." I feel thoroughly frantic and sock in with the telephone. I hit my peak of stress when put on hold with a static radio in my ear. But, finally, we do straighten it all out.

* * *

Thursday I go to a lady who is just the right person to work with on hypnosis and visualization. My high speed voice slows down, my humor and creativity are engaged. I create a glorious, goofy volleyball team made up of parts of myself that will constitute my inner support system. My deepest sense of power and wonder comes when she asks who the captain of this team is and the name comes in a flash: Daphne Vera Vivian. Let me explain who she is.

Two days after I was born, I contracted pneumonia and several fine Boston doctors conceded regretfully that there was no way I could survive, so great was the damage to my lungs. But that little baby kept hanging in there.

I was named off-handedly when my distraught lawyer father told my ailing mother that the legal deadline for naming the baby had arrived. A visitor in the room at the time advised naming me after friends. My mother rattled off three names: Daphne, Vera, and Vivian.

I continued to live against all odds, although the scar tissue allowed only panting. The doctors said that even if I managed to keep going, it would be some years before I could breathe normally. Then, one day, my mother came into the nursery and thought I was dead because she couldn't hear me panting: I was breathing normally! No one could explain why. Later my name was legally changed to Judy, but it was Daphne Vera Vivian who made that thrust for life. She knows how to lead me now.

*   *   *

Dr. Oncologist and Dr. Bone Marrow change the plan: the bone marrow harvest will be put off until January. I feel like a kid who has been let off a half hour early from detention. I leave John to cope with nerve-wracking reports from the insurance company that I am not covered. We assume that it is due to our signing up for a "better deal" to have separate policies, coincidentally going into effect when my cancer was diagnosed. It is a case of the right computer not knowing what the left computer is doing, but it takes John's good patience and skill to sort it out.

I prepare myself psychologically for the portacath implant and the first seventy-two-hour stint of chemotherapy which takes place in the hospital from Tuesday through Saturday, November 14-18. There will be six seventy-two-hour hospital chemo stints, spread over about as many months. At the end of that time radiation treatment will probably be done. If my blood count is okay, the second chemo may take place beginning December 6. I especially appreciate mail during these long treatment times. Phone calls and visits depend on how I'm feeling at a given moment. I will leave hospital treatment dates on our answering machine.

I continue to appreciate the powerful support of my doctors, nurses, family, friends, and psyche. There's room in my arena for anyone who wants to be present, in whatever role your skills and fantasy suggest—strategists, coaches, cheerleaders, game schedulers, waterbearers, fans—whatever, and only if it's right for you.

Thanks for joining me on the court where Daphne Vera Vivian heads my inner team.

Love, Judy

Dear Reader,

Today thinking about this letter on my morning walk, I noticed I was talking aloud. And while my tendency to become a street mutterer makes me a little nervous, my vocalizing seemed altogether appropriate to my mental process. I was exploring the subjects of affirmations, hypnotic writing, and the development of a calm, positive, reassuring, affectionate inner voice. I suppose these are three subjects, but for me one flows into another and they interact. Any one of them alone may be useful to you, or feel free to mix and match, or invent forms that spring naturally out of them for you.

*　　*　　*

Affirmations are short positive statements that you can say, write, sing, or chant. What we say in our mind can affect our feelings, experience, and physical well-being. Habitual negative and fearful statements sometimes chatter along in our heads without our conscious intention. We can choose to offer ourselves helpful and healing messages to gradually replace them. Some people who do affirmations notice significant changes in their feelings and experience, and feel that they promote physical healing. Usually affirmations are phrased in the present tense, which indicates that what we are stating is already so.

My surgeon said a wonderfully reassuring thing one day, when fluids built up after surgery, and I kept his sentence for repeated use: "This is 'Ho Hum' rather than 'Gee Whiz.'"

Other examples:

I receive healing from every source.
The chemo (radiation, or fill in the blank) is licking the cancer.
I am centered and confident.
My body and mind are a powerful healing team.
I am already healing.
I need live only with thisness, not with unknown, fearfully imagined thatness.
This is all I need to do for now.
The way I'm doing this is my right way to do it.
The choices I'm making are the right choices for me.
I invite my unconscious to continue my healing.

Generally people advise keeping affirmations in the present, but you might have noticed in the previous letter that I used the future tense in my series of affirmations to help prepare myself for looking at my breastless chest. This future was just overnight, and I was speaking directly to my unconscious to take over the task during sleep. The repeated "will" was also gently hypnotic, at once a suggestion to my will and an affirmation of my power to do what I needed to do. This is a good example of adapting forms to my own style. Do what works for you.

*   *   *

Hypnotic writing is my own name for my seat-of-the-pants letting my pencil guide me along into a trance, usually by allowing a lot of repetition, repetition with variations, letting rhythm develop naturally, using the hypnotic phrase "more and more," and sometimes making an open-ended invitation to something, such as relaxation, sleep, or the unconscious, to help me.

You can write strings of sentences in paragraph form. You can use the participle (*-ing*) form and use a new line for each statement, as I do in the example below. For me, using repetition, rhythm and the participle creates a soft, fluid quality that lures, lulls, and fixes my attention better than traditional affirmations.

Here's a fragment from such a writing. I did it the night before seeing my surgeon for a needle biopsy. The whole thing might be a bore to anyone but the writer, but don't worry about that. Your only reader is your mind, which is developing a calming trance. It loves soothing repetitions and rhythms. As you write, you may come up with new healing phrases and ideas. You may also develop an image that fixes your attention the more you let it evolve.

Feeling deeply my health.
Feeling the life force of optimism now.
Feeling my power of inner freedom.
Letting go of whatever I do not need.
Daring whatever I need to dare.
Embracing whatever I need to embrace.
Forgiving whatever and whomever I need to forgive.
Reaching out however I need to reach out.
Reaching inside however I need to reach inside.
Allowing myself to receive.
Being deeply with myself.
Being deeply with the universe.
Being deeply in Life.
From some centered place deep within,
Asking the body to be free of cancer.
Asking for a deep connection to healing:
Here, Now.

* * *

A self-supportive inner voice can develop over time and every kindliness and understanding you offer yourself contributes to its growth and power. As you talk to yourself, this voice will learn how to talk to you.

I realized the presence of such a voice in the early days of the first cancer. Driving along, I heard myself say in my head: "This is Judy's voice. This is my voice. It is not one of my characters." I was thinking of "voice" in relation to being a writer of fiction and the excitement that comes when one of my characters fully takes on its own distinctive voice and flows out of me. Suddenly I realized that this Judy voice of mine had a power that could support and serve me in the crisis of cancer.

As you talk to yourself in your head, use your own name freely, or a nickname people who love you use or used when you were a child. I sometimes affectionately address myself as "Kid," and thought I had met an inner voice embodied when my radiation oncologist called me "Kiddo." Now his "Kiddo" has become another part of my inner voice. In my experience, the best medical wizards serve up their brews laced with love. You *can* have it all! Recognize, seek, and receive love from outside *and* administer it liberally from within, and you will enhance your body's healing powers.

You may feel a little foolish at first, but a good starter and frequent fill-in is "I love you, (Your Name)." I cannot tell you how often I said, "I love you, Judy," to myself—before surgeries, coming out of anesthesia, during chemos, before or during any event or time that particularly aroused anxiety, and often just for good measure before going to sleep each night or on waking in the morning.

You might try affirmations, hypnotic phrases, or self-love messages individually or overlapping. You can do them in your head or aloud, accompanied by movement, or/and music—sort of free form dance-exercise. You can write them. You can say or chant them when driving alone. You can sing them. If you are artistic, you can probably draw or model healing images of love.

Remember that nobody has to see or hear your words, so you can even say such messages in your head when you're in a waiting room or during a procedure. I talked to myself in my head when I didn't have the advantage of an anxiety-busting conversation with a medical person. I sometimes even carried on inner and outer conversations at once—presumably keeping them separate! I may talk out loud to myself in the street, but I certainly knew enough to monitor vocalization in the hospital. After all, I didn't want anybody transferring me to the psychiatric floor and forgetting about chemo!

Here's to your becoming adept at talking to yourself. And if by any chance somebody hears you muttering and asks, "What?", just answer in a gently chiding voice, "I was talking to myself. Don't you know it's rude to eavesdrop?"

Love, Judy

January 1

Dear Friends,

Some of you report you missed receiving my first letter. That's because I sent it only to people I hadn't notified in person. If you're papering your wall with the oeuvre of Judy Hart, of course you may have a copy.

Before I tell you more about my adventure, let me tell you that your response has been extraordinary. When you learned that I had no button-down-the-front clothes and could not pull tops over my head after the mastectomy, you got me buttoned shirts. You have made and delivered food. You have driven me to appointments. You have run errands for me. You have cleaned my house and done my laundry. You arranged to have a property-line fence at my bedroom window built while I was in the hospital, so the noise wouldn't bother me. You put a notice about me in the newsletter of a cancer research foundation and sent along huge packets of get well wishes from its readers. You telephone, sometimes from great distance. You send packages and leave things on my doorstep: resource information, favorite books, stuffed animals, plants and flowers, soaps, herb teas, scarves, slippers, pajamas, to name a few! You respond to my symbolism and give me a paper garland of toy soldiers for my battle and a daphne shrub, not only because you know I love the fragrant plant, but because now its name carries special meaning.

You, who realize my mailing list is long, send me stamps. You put names and addresses on your computer and make labels for these letters. You, who realize my long distance phone bills are second only to the medical bills, send telephone gift certificates. You, who know your friend is a rubber stamp addict, shamelessly encourage my vice by showering me with rubber stamps. You design and crochet a jacket of many colors for hospital and daily use, and wildly creative hats to cover my almost hairless head. You, who have received mistletoe from my past annual treks in the countryside, now give me mistletoe. You decorate my Christmas tree.

And you send the most delightful variety of get-well cards and letters that I imagine any one person has ever received. You share your reactions to my illness and letters and tell me some of your meanings. You tell me that my relationship to my situation has helped you to look at your life and get clarity. You enter into my volleyball image, tell me your volleyball experiences, literal and metaphorical, and come up with what role you want to play for yourself and for me. So you see, you are an extraordinary lot.

We are all an extraordinary lot when we reach beyond what we know of ourselves in the ordinary course of things and find how much richness we have to draw from. A magical part of the human story is being lived here, and all of you who read these letters participate in it. So would you care to join me again on my voyage?

My first three-day stint of chemotherapy in November is preceded by surgery to place a portacath under my skin near my left shoulder. The next day, the chemo is started. An IV (intravenous) pole holding two pumps and several bags of liquids becomes my constant companion. The chemo is released evenly and steadily, one for twenty-four hours, another for seventy-two hours. A third one is given as one shot. The pump is plugged into a wall outlet, but also works on batteries, so I unplug myself to go to the bathroom or perambulate, a rare fashion plate in hospital johnny, pink long johns, crocheted jacket, and zany hat.

Seventy-two hours gets long. Anti-nausea medication helps some-what, but I often experience an undefinable malaise. Though I have tapes and books, they usually feel like too much noise or work. Especially too much noise is my roommate's television. I am fortunate in that a private room becomes available halfway through my first stint and for all of my second one.

But there are also little events that stimulate my imagination and lift my spirits. The nurses in this unit are all A+, and what a variety of person-alities and humorous exchanges! I am blessed with doctors with a ready sense of humor. Even the equipment has personality. The talkative pumps beep to communicate. The first time one beeps to indicate that air bubbles are in the tube, both John and I blanch. After all, we know from TV thrillers that bad guys murder patients by shooting air into their veins. We are relieved to learn that it takes a good deal more air than a few bubbles. And then there's the light under the bed. A light under the bed? Uh oh—some hallucinatory side effect nobody told me about. Doctors and nurses confirm my sensory experience and join in fanciful explanations of its purpose: I should be lying under my bed to read at night maybe?

*   *   *

A couple of weeks after the first chemo, my hair starts to fall out, and in three days it disperses everywhere. It coats the bathtub and clogs the drain. It settles on clothing, skin, furniture, pillows, bedsheets, floor. It seems we have a shedding pet yak in the house. I am disbelieving when I find hair in my toothbrush. In my *toothbrush*? How can the pet yak have gotten in my toothbrush?

I am racing time as the ordered wig has not come and I have to get a wig elsewhere fast. It looks stiff and awkward on me. My haircutter helps to make it look better. But even after all the effort, my problem is not solved. The wig is hot, itchy, and bothersome over the ears. It requires continual primping and doesn't feel like me. Fortunately, at the wig shop I also purchased turbans. The bright ones—red and hot pink—aren't bad. They're soft and comfortable. They look better when I add a colorful snake pin front and center, though now I look like a member of some new religious sect. I look into scarves. Most fabrics, if worn over the ears, make such a racket I can't hear properly. I tie the scarf so my ears stick out. Oops: I seem to show an instantaneous and substantial drop in IQ. Silk is too slippery. Finally, in an Indian store I find loosely woven, soft cotton scarves. Though I can't try them on as my departing hair would coat the cloth, a couple of scarves held above my head look as though they would work.

At home I cry a little for my lost hair. I storm about the nuisance of being unable to go out of the house without something on my head and having to think about it not clashing violently with the rest of my clothing. I'm not made for these problems of haute couture. Rescue comes when a friend designs and crochets imaginative hats. She feels challenged by the problem of how to replace the fullness lost by the absence of hair. Once I have a couple of things I can wear, I'm over the hump and enjoy my new headgear.

*   *   *

The nadir has arrived, the predictable low-energy point seven to ten days after chemo. I took fright when I first heard this dread word used medically. I associated the nadir with astronomy, mythology, and meta-phor. I imagined myself like a cartoon dog, belly flattened to the floor, rump in the air and eyes rolling. The reality is nowhere near as daunting as the word, but I am in a spacey, unathletic state when I go for my first appointment with a man skilled in acupuncture and Chinese herbs. Several friends have suggested this adjunct treatment. For some patients, it helps reduce nausea and raise energy and white cell count.

The office is in a picket-fenced Victorian house with outside wooden stairways, little brick paths, and the air of a dollhouse set down in the midst of real life.

In the hushed interior, one quietly imposing wall is lined with shelves of see-through plastic boxes containing herbs. Each is labeled with Chinese characters and English renderings as mysterious as *Mook Yok, Sing Ma, Jee Sut,* and *Chen Pay.* A gentle foreign odor pervades the office. A computer sits on the desk. I am asked about my medical situation, have my pulse taken in several places on both wrists, and my tongue inspected. As we talk, the herbalist writes in Chinese characters the names of the herbs he'll select. Then he and an assistant, who has been sitting in on the interview, go to the plastic boxes, extract, and weigh the herbs on delicate brass hand scales. I divide them and put half in each of two brown paper bags. In my nadir haze, I go home with my bags of herbs, directions for brewing, and bemused wonder at the world I've entered.

Now, these herbs do not resemble oregano or marjoram. They're mostly large pieces—fungi, sticks, things that look like handmade tongue depressors, others like nettles. John says the collection looks like what you might find caught in the trees after a flood, including remains of bird nests.

The brewing fills the house with unaccustomed, not wholly welcome smells. The drink tastes—Oh, my God—it tastes *dreadful.* Remember,

Judy, the herbalist said that some people find it unpalatable initially, and suggested taking small sips. It usually gets better. He told me that a week later, one woman couldn't fathom how she could have found them disagreeable. A *week*? At the pace I'm going, I'll be sipping all day and I'm not sure I can stand to spend such a shuddery week. The second cup is already better. I'm astonished. And by the next day, it's no problem. Not something you'd cheat on your diet for, but no problem.

Two friends ask to taste. The first spits it into the sink pronto, her features showing every sign of trauma. "Ouf. That stuff is terrible with a capital *T*." The other tastes and quietly agrees, tipping her head back in mental search. "There's something familiar here from my childhood." (She was brought up in Egypt.) "Could have been a soup. But," she adds, "it's certainly not one that would have made the hostess popular."

Accustomed now to the taste, I'm nonetheless irritated by the nuisance of the brewing. It seems I measure out the liquid time after time and there's still way too much, and then the next time it has almost boiled away. I swear and storm at the annoyance of this every-three-day task. I play hookey for one round. As I leave for my herbalist appointment, I say to John, "Well, I've had my resistance and *I do not like doing this*, but perhaps it's not a bad thing to have *one* thing I hate doing."

John bursts out laughing. "There's nothing else, of course, that could fit that description?" he queries. "Little things like surgeries and chemotherapy?" I leave for the herbalist laughing. When I tell the tale to a friend, she builds on it. "What a wonderful arena to express anger: 'Those *+<%$#! herbs!'" I am so busy preparing myself to go through surgeries and chemo as comfortably as possible, and to go *with* them rather than against them, that anger at them does not arise. After this awareness, I feel friendlier toward the herbs, they seem to cause less trouble brewing, and I think they may be playing a part in my doing so well.

*   *   *

Chemo knocks white cells down. The second chemo has to be delayed a week because my cell count is only 2,000. The oncologist wants 3,500-4,000. After some hypnotic suggestion to bring them up and aiming for a higher number, I find myself singing to whatever music I hear "I have 5,000 white cells." I try Christmas carols. Wowie. One is made to order: "Joy to the world: I have five thou; I have five thousand white cells." The words fit all the way through the verse. Driving along in the car, I belt it out or fit the words to a tape of Irish hammered dulcimer music. Like any other song one hears too often, the words go on repeating in my head. Well, I got 3,600. Enough to go to chemo. John is grateful I didn't make 5,000. "You would have tied up the phone for hours telling everybody. You'd have been stopping strangers in the street. 3,600. Phew! That's fine, Jude."

*   *   *

Over the course of one week I have encounters with two people that bring me close to cancer deaths. I am shaken and spend some time processing, then set it aside.

I go to my hypnotherapist. I am ready to ask who the enemy on the other side of the volleyball net is. I drop into hypnosis and an image emerges: some squatters have drifted onto my land and their ominous, darkly clad, invisible-faced leader, named Stryker (Strike her?), knocks on my door. After some good work, I tire and need to leave them. I sigh and say how much I just want to be carried for a little bit. My hypnotherapist offers me the image of a peaceful path to walk on and suggests someone coming toward me who will carry me. I see a hazy figure. As it draws closer, I perceive it is enveloped in dark clothing and the face is too receded in a hood to see. Suddenly I get very upset. "No," I shout. "I don't want *this one* to carry me."

"Is it Death?" she asks.

"Yes, it is. And I don't want it. I don't want it. I don't want it!"

The imagery stops like a film in a single frame as we face off in the path, the figure impassive, I crying and expressing my refusal.

"Is there anyone from your team who might join you?" she asks.

Suddenly a little tyke of a girl takes my left hand. Daphne Vera Vivian has joined me. A patient, wise, gray-haired woman glides up on my right

61

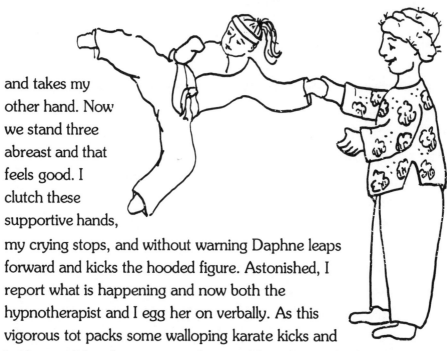

and takes my other hand. Now we stand three abreast and that feels good. I clutch these supportive hands, my crying stops, and without warning Daphne leaps forward and kicks the hooded figure. Astonished, I report what is happening and now both the hypnotherapist and I egg her on verbally. As this vigorous tot packs some walloping karate kicks and bashes with her fists, my own legs and fists join in the fray. Eventually her action subsides, so I, too, stop and wait to see what will happen. The woman on my right speaks in a firm, quiet, hypnotic voice. "Turn around," she intones. "Just turn around and walk the other way." She repeats this many times with small variations and great persistence. To my astonishment, the figure slowly turns, as if in a trance, and begins to walk away. My wise lady keeps up her chanting directive, and the three of us move along the path, herding him away. When he moves far enough off, the scene fades; I come out of the trance and feel enormously better. I did not realize how much the suggestions of cancer death had weighed on me. I feel much freer now that I have given my fear full expression and had such a life-affirming encounter.

*   *   *

A couple of weeks after my second chemo, I walk into a hypnotherapy session, saying, "Today I want to go after those cancer cells." I drop into hypnosis and continue the exploration of the dark-clad man, named Stryker, and acknowledge him as somehow involved in starting the cancer. As we talk to him, he seems not to be an entirely negative figure, but he has been using his energy on the wrong side. He has a steel rod in the center of his torso, and as we talk it becomes available to use in my behalf against the cancer cells. Now my torso and arms hum with energy. I emerge from the trance into this power. I take a huge stick and hit a convenient mattress with now *Striker* force, feeling myself whap those cancer cells. I beat with gusto until I collapse in laughter, feeling toned and fraught with accomplishment.

*   *   *

I dream that someone is trying to reach "Encino." Though I know nobody by that name, I sense maybe she is connected to me and so I ask her last name and how I can help the caller get in touch with her.

Encino is Spanish for live oak. Like other oaks, it is sturdy and hardy. Unlike other oaks, it is evergreen. How wonderful that a part of me is calling to connect to another sturdy, hardy, evergreen live oak in me! I want to help these two parts to connect. Working on the dream in my journal late one evening, I end with: *Now here in the peaceful lighted candle and Christmas tree night, I invite you both to make yourselves more known to me. I will welcome your development. I thank the unconscious for this gift and invite it to reveal more.*

*   *   *

I revel in Christmas: the wrapping, the cards, the visits. I go to a publication party for an anthology in which one of my short stories appears. I play games with a family on New Year's Eve. John and I both get the flu.

January brings me back to medical necessities: two rounds of giving blood for the bone marrow harvest, meeting the doctor who will do that surgery, and blood tests to check the progress of the white cells.

The date of the surgery is changed by one day. John calls to make sure the insurance watchdogs, who have to okay each hospital admittance, have the new surgery date and know that chemo will follow it. He talks a moment, then his jaw drops in a stunned silence. He speaks again: "I would hardly initiate this on my own." When he hangs up, I ask him what that was all about. "She asked if the doctors knew about the change of date. I should have said, 'No. It was all my idea. I thought surgery and chemo would be a nice change from dinner and the theater for my wife's upcoming birthday, and this would be a better date for us!'"

Well, we've decided to inform the doctors and invite them along. So far, they've been darn good company.

Love, Judy

Dear Reader,

One of my fundamental ways of looking at things is that we are made up of many inner parts and that it is possible to identify them and relate to them in a kindly, supportive way.

It's natural, therefore, for me to relate the same way to parts of my body. My best way of handling the impersonality and terror of medical fact is to personalize parts of the body and physical states.

In this letter I want to offer ways to support your body or body parts that are hurting. In the next letter I will address the subject of writing or talking to your emotional parts.

There are many ways to practice your own healing activities. For example, Norman Cousins encountered his disease magnificently, using his fine investigative and rational talents. He learned so much about his disease that he was able to ask subtle technical questions and make suggestions to his doctor that were incorporated into his treatment. But if I had to do it Norman Cousins' way, I'd feel as though I were taking exams in my most stressful kind of college course. I also have trouble with some directions for visualization. They are often too literal, too scientifically or physiologically based, or too masculine for me. When I try to follow them, I get stuck in good-girl, get-your-homework-done labor without meaning. But if you are more rationally and scientifically oriented, by all means make use of those admirable skills. And perhaps you can draw from very different sides of yourself. Trust that the best way for you will keep emerging.

You can address your body as a whole or any part that has been invaded by cancer or treatment. You can even address a body part that has been removed. In treatment for my first cancer, I did not lose a breast. Even the lumpectomy scar was unnoticeable. But in the second cancer, I talked in my head to and cuddled my breasts before losing them and wrote in my journal about my resistance to losing them. I never wrote specifically to them. Perhaps I wasn't ready, or other needs came too thick and fast.

Here are three journal excerpts relating to the loss of my lymph nodes that I wrote over a period of several weeks during the first cancer. Keep in mind that each is the extracted core of a long, sprawling writing session.

If you choose to write, honor the sprawl. Something anchoring and calming seems to come from spending time with yourself in this way. And often, you'll get a nugget—a new piece of understanding, a shift in perception, a bit of comfort or reassurance, as I did in each of these writings. Notice that, for me, the shifts toward comfort happen when an image emerges and I get absorbed in its development. You might also notice that the very act of speaking to my body or body part keeps me aware that I am larger than my distressed part.

* * *

The first journal entry was written prior to the removal of my lymph nodes:

"What's up, Psyche? What's bothering? And who is it that's bothered? This is nowhere near as big a deal surgically as the hysterectomy, and for that you felt so centered that the night before the operation, I danced in my hospital room, then sailed through the surgery in a way that astonished my medical helpers."

Hmm . . . Something's coming about why I felt centered for that surgery, and how this is different . . . I've got it.

"It's not your psyche. This is me, your Body speaking. I'm the one who's upset. This is not like the other operation. I welcomed that, because I'd taken a helluva beating for a long time. We'd tried everything else without success. We were ready. It was good riddance.

"But this, I don't get. These lymph nodes don't storm around causing trouble. They're quiet and well behaved. They do their job. And you're telling me we're going to turn them over to a hit man. And furthermore, all of us expect to find out they're innocent of dealing cancer and don't deserve to be done in. Now, what kind of sense does that make?"

"Of course it doesn't make sense to you. Thanks for speaking up. Look, we're pretty sure the cancer's out, but if it has traveled like an elm bark beetle inside the tree, the whole tree can go kaput.

"That's all of you.

"That's all of me.

"That's Us, Good Body Tree.

"So, we give up a branch, a twig, some lymph nodes to find out if any beetles have set forth. And if, by chance, they have, then we know we have to set to and squelch 'em proper.

"You are the All-Star Hero going out on a life-protecting mission. You'll have some discomforts as heros on missions do, but nothing major, nothing you can't handle.

"And listen, Body Friend: we have a secret partnership, you and I. We're old hands at this business of healing. I'll be with you all the way."

*   *   *

The next writing was to help reassure myself when I was recovering from lymph node surgery:

My arm feels weird since the surgery. In my distaste, I've been dissociating myself from it, the very part that needs my help and encouragement.

So, now I acknowledge that I'm afraid about the future of this estranged and lonely arm. To what extent will it return to normal? How many of its present peculiarities are here to stay?

I love you, sweet arm. You are the receiver of the shock of sur-

70

gery. It's okay to be a little uncertain who you are just now. You're not used to the odd twinges that feel like tape being pulled slowly off where there is no tape. Your nerves have been altered and you and they don't know each other now.

We all worry when unchosen, unfamiliar personalities come into our lives: a new colleague, neighbor, or in-law. If we're not immediately drawn to this unknown other, we may imagine a future of friction and we're afraid of being stuck with 'em. Yeah. That's it, isn't it? You're afraid of being stuck with someone incompatible. These nerve fellows aren't the old reliables who worked here before the surgery. They zing around. They're odd-ball, like someone whose sense of humor jars you. They're new guys on the job, not yet sure of their capacities. They, too, got hurtled into a position they didn't choose, but they're plucky, adaptable fellows with an ability to learn.

Please let me introduce you. Left Arm, these are the Nerve Fellows. Nerve Fellows, this is Left Arm. It's okay if you don't feel immediately at home together. I'll help you get acquainted and build trust in each other, 'cuz I think rather highly of you both. You have a right to feel battered and uncertain just now. Your confidence will grow as you feel my deep confidence in you. Come. Let me give you a temporary one-armed hug which will soon be replaced by the full two-armed Judy special. Receive my love and relax as you go about learning the ropes of your new work.

I discovered my finger bleeding when I was at the theater on a Saturday night. I wrote the following when I hit a moment of panic about being without the protection of lymph nodes:

I think my surgeon said that without lymph nodes, even an ordinary break in the skin would be cause for antibiotics. I made the decision to stay for the play and seek further medical clarification after the weekend, but I cried on the way home and I'm in high distress. I'm scared of my future if such an ordinary occurrence endangers me physically or sends me into panic. I desperately wished I'd paid more attention and asked if I needed to keep antibiotics on hand and take them for something as minor as this.

Now it is time to honor my feelings of loss and vulnerability, my fear, and aloneness. I've shared my tears and fears with John, but it is here on this paper and in this deepest self that I encounter my loss. It is in this act of writing that I shall forge a transformation that will make my fears transitory.

I didn't grieve for those lost lymph nodes. How could I? I had no relationship to them. Their removal is not like losing an arm or a leg . . . or a breast. Until now, I've been chiefly aware of all I have not lost that I could have lost. I've been aware of how fortunate I am in the limits of this cancer.

I salute you, warm tears and tender feelings. I bow my head respectfully as at a graveside for your brave and honorable death, lymph nodes. I pay tribute to the daily service you performed. Like a boss with a exquisite secretary, I took your skills for granted. I understood you no better than the boss understands the squiggles of shorthand or the tact and savvy required to wangle his business arrangements without a hitch. Henceforth, I must be more attentive and savvy on my own. Your passing gives me intense appreciation of ordinary functions.

So now I turn to you, dear bereaved relatives, extant sister nodes, and other anonymous workers in my body. You, too, are exquisite, even if I don't understand the ins and outs of how you earn your living. Tonight let us go back to the house together for a funeral collation. Tonight let us toast the departed. We thank them for their gift of hallelujah information about the limits of the cancer. We shall miss them, and become inventive as we learn to live without them. And we shall do whatever is necessary, these parts of the body and the psyche which form a royal We. We are at once a collection of state and an individual responsibly forging along alone. And unlike Queen Victoria, We shall be amused, because We have a rich capacity to replace a lost part with some previously unimagined hairpin and carry on the functions of state.

* * *

You can also talk or write to physical states such as shock, fatigue, wooziness, malaise, sleeplessness, nausea, pain, returning energy, increased mobility, and the hum of good health. When sick in bed with chemo or sluffing off effects of surgery medication, I would often talk lovingly and supportively in my head to my body, a body part, or a body state. I'd relate to it as a mother might to a sick child, offering calming reassurance.

If you're feeling well enough, drawing, scribbling lines, or using colors might work well, too. Dance, movement, or singing could express any kind of feeling, and could also celebrate increasing energy or mobility. Don't forget the value of celebrating the positive! And just imagining physical expression might help you, as it did me once, when in the shadowy half-world of medication.

In a category all its own is the cancer, or *your* cancer, depending on how you see it. In this case, a different approach is needed. Rather than supporting it, you might imagine it as a part out of whack, wanting something from you to help it quiet down, transform, and heal.

Whatever way you find to be there for your body is what will help you most. If you feel angry that your body has betrayed you or estranged from it because it is hurting you, you may want to shine your light on that anger or sense of betrayal. And you don't have to take an either/or stand.

You may be able to acknowledge *both* your hurt, angry, betrayed, estranged feelings *and* a desire to help your body.

Here's to your finding your own natural ways of being supportive toward your body.

Love, Judy

February 10

Dear Friends,

On with the tale! It is time to meet the doctor who specializes in bone marrow harvest and transplant. Bone marrow harvest is a simple procedure, similar to the bone marrow biopsy I had. I am to lie on my stomach while this doctor and my oncologist each work on the back of one hip, extracting bone marrow with a needle. Unlike the biopsy, it will take about an hour and I will have a general anesthesia. Surgery is scheduled for January 18, followed by my third three-day course of chemo. I'm not looking forward to this double event.

I did a pretty good job of putting all this on the fringes of my mind when it was explained before. It makes sense to harvest my bone marrow, which keeps frozen for years. I've seen it as insurance if I find myself in deeper trouble with a recurrence. I hope to hell I'll never have to use it.

Now suddenly this doctor is breaking through my defenses. Experimentally the procedure is being done for breast cancer at an earlier stage. By not waiting until the cancer has spread—but when the risk of spread is high—there is some indication that high-dose chemo followed by bone marrow transplant raises the chances of killing off all the cancer and getting home free without recurrence. "We don't have a protocol for this yet," he says—and by "we" he means doctors all over the country—"but I'm going to a meeting in Colorado, and in about six weeks I should be able to come to you with information and we can consider whether this is something to offer you to be done in the next couple of months."

Bingo. I go into Shockland again. It's not until much later that I realize this is not the first time I've heard about this. My oncologist mentioned it in our first meeting, but because it was experimental and because I was busy going into shock over the news of the estrogen receptors and bone marrow harvest, I let it go by very fast.

At the end of the session, John points to the doctor's graph and says it looks like an artist's drawing on a restaurant tablecloth. Sometimes, then the artist signs the cloth and a lucky diner walks away with a valuable piece of art. This genial doctor scrawls a signature, rips off the graph, and hands it to John, who pockets it with pleasure and amusement. He feels it was a good interview. I agree, but tell him I've gone into shock again and need him to hang by.

I have an hour and a half to wait before returning to have my second pint of blood drawn, which will be given back to me after the bone marrow harvest. As I am normally happy waiting and socializing in the hospital, and John gets restive, our plan was for him to leave after the doctor's appointment and return to pick me up after the blood draw. Instead he takes my arm and we go to the cafeteria. It is the lunch hour, and the room teeming with people is not solidly grounded for me. The advantage of such a crowd, however, is that I see four or five people I know, and from my hanging-onto-John teetering state, I start to use my people resources. The special clinical cancer nurse is eating with colleagues, and I greet her and tell her what I've just come from. "I'll come over to your table when I finish," she says, and I can feel a thin but distinct lifeline attach to me. Soon she comes to sit, puts a hand on my shoulder, and listens empathically and helpfully. I feel better after her visit, but the dining room still shimmers and pulsates, and I continue to lean close to John.

I spot my surgeon in his operating-room greens, standing conferring with his secretary. I know they are deeply engaged, but I go up and give him a friendly poke in the back and get two friendly grins that strengthen my lifeline a little more.

On the way to have my blood drawn, fortified by food and human lifelines, I stop to see a new acquaintance in Admittance, one who has only just read my letters. For a moment I live in the reality of my writing and people's warm reactions to it and me, then I head downstairs to be greeted by the now familiar nurses in the "Phabulous Pheresis Phacility," as their computer banner announces. I am out of shock.

Procedure finished and waiting on the curb for John to drive out of the garage, I once again wonder how I landed in this Reno gambling saloon with my health. I also understand how sick people can resent the well. As I stand there, I honor that deep awareness and the resentment that I feel in this moment. How glad I'd be to settle for the pack of complaints we all grouch about in the ordinary course of things.

But if I had the choice, would I trade who I am or the rest of what I have in order to be out of this situation? Resounding no. Almost every-body has some major problem(s), just different. The feeling shifts. By the time I'm riding home with John, I start to fantasize: "Hey, you know if I could trade this situation for standing in line at the post office, the super-market, *and* the Department of Motor Vehicles—after a long, frustrating search for a parking place—I'd do it in a snap, for three weeks running, if that were the condition of the trade. Yep. If that would take care of this whole bone marrow issue, *post office here I come!*"

* * *

The bone marrow doctor noticed I had a birthday coming up and commented that so did he. In fact, the date is the day for which my bone marrow harvest has been scheduled.

I go to Pre-Op Testing. I know my way. I know the procedures. I know the people. After covering my list of questions and requests, includ-ing one for my anesthesiologist, I say to the nurse, "I have a question you may not have heard before."

"Unlikely, Judy," she says, shaking her head, "but let's hear it."

"I want to know if there's a way, consistent with the need for a sterile field, to write 'Happy Birthday!' to my doctor on my backside."

"Número uno," she answers. "Nobody has asked that one before. And it's easily done. I'll give you a special pen surgeons use to mark the body. Have your husband do it before you leave the house tomorrow morning."

Before our 5:30 a.m. departure, John letters my backside in pizzazzy purple. Despite my playfulness, I feel anxious when, for the first time, my body balks during surgery preparations. Even the smell of the soap in the bathroom makes me feel ill. It is not until I'm in the final holding room, sharing my backside with the anesthesiologist, that I lose my malaise. Now as I laugh and relate, I feel myself calming. As John wrote a bit higher than the surgical field and I do not know where I'll be draped, I charge the anesthesiologist with making sure the message is seen by the birthday doctor.

Some hours after the surgery, it is the non-birthday doctor who comes first to see me. I ask if they got my message. "Indeed we did and we wrote one back. You'll have to get a mirror."

For a mirror, I use my nurse. She reads "Happy Harvest and No Returns." Thank you, purple-penned prose. Thank you for giving me a project during an uncomfortable time and for ripples of laughter from a whole line of medical helpers.

81

It's a long haul coming out of the anesthesia, a long woozy day. I recall that after the mastectomy, my body finally sluffed it off in the wee hours of the following morning. I propose to my body and my unconscious that somewhere between 2 and 4 a.m. I will feel better. At 3 a.m. I recognize the change. At 5 I am awake, feeling good, and looking to enjoy the two or three hours before the chemo begins. Actually I'm pretty comfortable for about the first ten hours of chemo. Then I start to be sick, and from then on am sick more than the previous times, so I have more anti-nausea medication, which means more wooziness and an all-around more taxing time.

One night in the bathroom, I feel as if I am about to faint and have to push the "Help" button. My kindly nurse puts a chair in front of me and drapes the upper part of my seated body over it. All I can think of is the huge impossible distance back to bed. Even with help, I'm too light-headed to stand. I continue draped there, feeling unreal and muddled as two more nurses arrive to help carry me out of the bathroom. The three of them hoist me and lay me flat on the floor beside my bed. Then six perfectly synchronized, gentle hands lift my body back onto the bed. I have been returned to the castle after frightening travels in foreign lands. I am awash with gratitude for being lifted so exquisitely effectively, so exquisitely lovingly, by three fellow beings when I could not fend for myself. It is a powerful, luminous human experience. Afterward my nurse stays beside me, stroking and talking soothingly and hypnotically, acknowledging the scariness of almost fainting. Gently she invites me to let go into a safe and comfortable place.

*　　*　　*

I am very weak and it occurs to me that maybe it is worth trying some food. The doctor agrees and says he'll arrange to have the dietician come and see me.

Dietician? Dietician? Not the cook? Ah, not the cook. Memory swoops me back to 1962 when I spent three months in a tiny hospital in a small Mexican town recovering from hepatitis. I had many adventures there. One involved the hospital cook, Mariquita. She would have had me eating a spicy Mexican diet if she'd had her way. "It's because of our *picante* food that we have so little cancer," she told me proudly. Hepatitis, however, was rampant. The only town doctor, a Spanish émigré and friend, asked a mutual American friend, who'd had hepatitis, to make up a week's worth of appropriately bland, fat-free menus. She submitted them to me and him for final revision. He then took them to Mariquita and went over each item to make sure she understood. He even educated her as to how to bake a potato, a concept foreign to the Mexican diet. The first baked potato that arrived was heaven, and I was pleased we'd scattered so many through the week's menus. But the second potato was a disaster:

stone cold and shriveled; Mariquita had failed to grasp that hot was an essential characteristic of the baked potato and had cooked and refrigerated enough to last the week. She thought such a detail hilarious, but good-naturedly was perfectly willing to begin again.

Plain boiled chicken was something I could tolerate, and I was astonished when she greeted me from my doorway one day, holding a live chicken by the legs and laughing, "*Aquí esta sú pollo.*"

A matronly woman in her forties, Mariquita expressed great concern for me—and for my mother. My poor mother! She must be worried sick to have her *angelito* so far from home. Mariquita vowed that she would look after me as only a mother could. At twenty-five, I couldn't imagine being anyone's *angelito,* but I was deeply touched by her warmth.

One morning, I was woken by Mariquita babbling hysterically by my side. "*Voy a morir,*" I caught. "I'm going to get hepatitis and die." I grappled my way to consciousness and tried to get hold of why she thought this would happen to her, but she only became more incoherent. I took another tack and tried at least to address her terror that she would die, pointing out that even if she got hepatitis, she would not die of it. "After all, I'm not dying of this disease." "You're rich," she countered. "You can afford to stay in the hospital." It was a point well taken, but not advancing my efforts in her behalf. (Incidentally, my private room cost $11 a day, less than my previous lodgings, at a time when American private hospital rooms ran about $35-$40 and my insurance covered a maximum of $21.) Suddenly intuition flashed me the source of Mariquita's terror. The doctor had explained to me how little understanding there was of infection and contagion. Part of his lesson in the kitchen was to state very firmly, that under no circumstances was anyone to eat food that returned on my trays—even if it looked untouched. I knew for a certainty that she had not heeded his warning, that he'd caught her in the act, and that he'd used the only method he felt sure would work to scare her from any further tasting.

I'm jarred back to the present by the arrival of the dietician. She is wearing a white coat and carries a clipboard. She is friendly and helpful. It's nice that the hospital has such a personable dietician, but, ah, I miss my cook, who looked after her *angelito*.

* * *

The other times I left the hospital almost immediately after the chemo was finished. This time I am too weak and woozy and am still confined to using a commode beside the bed. I am left with just the sugar-and-salt IV. I've had practically no food for five days, the few attempts to eat having made me sick. By Tuesday the IV is removed. I've stopped being sick, but the wooziness from the anti-nausea medication is still considerable. Gradually I start up the food chain of clear liquids to full liquids. Again I get the feeling that the wee hours will bring relief. In the interim I notice that I am mentally humming a song and seeing the matching Fred Astaire and Ginger Rogers dance steps. Something about the way the music opens out and out and out and then comes tumbling back to "I'm in heaven when we're dancing cheek to cheek," something about the way the dance shifts from a beautiful flowing movement to a vigorous tap routine, something about the graceful dancing body, helps me through this woozy waiting time. And then I hear my inner voice chanting, "Kill those cancer cells. Kill those cancer cells. I love you, Judy. It's gonna be all right. The anti-nausea medication is gonna disperse. I'm going to feel more and more stable, more and more secure, more and more solid. I love you, Judy. It's gonna be all right." Again I get the feeling that in the wee hours the wooziness will abate and, again, the timing talleys.

* * *

I feel well enough to pull out a twenty-fifth anniversary cartoon book of Peanuts that I picked up in the second hand bookstore before coming to the hospital. This is just the reading I can handle: clear lines, big pictures, color, affection. I can even read the text in which Charles Schultz talks about his origins and creativity. It feels wonderful to spend time in the presence of affection and the creative process. At times I am touched to tears. At first I don't pay any attention, because I've noticed at certain stages of chemo I sometimes have brief bouts of weeping, which seem to be more physiological than attached to any particular emotion. This time I sense there is a common trigger for my tears, and then, I have it. I cry when something I read points to the acceptance and encouragement of Schultz's creativity and his feelings of soundness when he is engaged in it.

Since turning forty, thirteen years ago, I have been engaged in a deep struggle to accept and nurture my creativity, battling and overcoming a scourging, paralyzing inner critic in order to be able to write. It is surely this slow, often painful fight that has forged the Judy who meets this cancer. It is ironic that now as the Furies are pursuing me, I write as never before. I have only begun to be modestly published. At times, I feel the pressure of time and wonder if my work will see print before I die. At others, I feel that my writing may quite literally help save my life. I have come through more than a decade of inner struggle that has given me riches that are mine to keep. And now I have come through this surgery and this chemo. I will surely be sprung from here in the morning.

But no. One more twist. With my discharge orders already given, I go into a sudden and frightening slump that turns out to be caused by a big drop in blood pressure. Though the doctor is still optimistic that it will rise and I'll be able to leave later in the day, I am anxious and discouraged. I'm again limited to using the commode beside the bed; the bathroom might as well be across the Pacific. I am perched there when my nurse comes in and says that because I was officially discharged, this room has been reassigned and they have to move me to a room with another patient. The effort of being moved seems overwhelming. Suddenly my mooring line slides out from under me. And there on the commode, I burst into tears of sheer physical weakness and despair and clasp my arms around the Patient Care Assistant who is attending me. She hugs me back and holds and strokes me and speaks in a mellifluous, rhythmic voice. "You'll go home today. You'll see. Doctor's not worried. You're gonna be all right. You'll see." She talks and strokes and I let my fear and distress out in tears and hug this close, nurturing human body. The crisis passes. I am grateful for not holding my feelings in and to the person who has supported me.

When the three people come to roll me into the other room, I again express my feelings. "This is a bummer." They pause, acknowledge my feelings and each lays a gentle hand on me. It is a moment of healing and letting go before the move.

By the time I'm in the other room, I realize my energy is coming back. My blood pressure is rising as predicted. It's gonna be all right. I will go home today. I've come through a week in the hospital under testing conditions. It's gonna be all right. I'm going home.

Love, Judy

Dear Reader,

If you stayed with me through that last letter telling of my most difficult chemo, it may have been hard for you. I want to remind you of two things: it does *not* mean that you are likely to have a similar experience, and if you do have one particularly tough chemo, it does *not* mean that all your others will be like it. All my others, before and after, although not my idea of a jolly time, were significantly easier. In addition, at whatever point you read these letters, protocols for bone marrow transplants will have been in place for a number of years and medical experience has been building since the era when the transplant option was offered to me.

I hope you also noticed in the last letter how much my assorted resources helped me through my hardest time. So now I want to share my thoughts about and suggestions for meeting the feelings that cancer diagnosis and treatment may arouse.

Just as it is possible to relate in a friendly, supportive way to parts of your body, I believe it can sometimes help to identify, receive, hear out, and, if appropriate, comfort your feelings. If what I'm saying is new to you, please don't think that you must learn to do all this overnight! Let the ideas and images wash over you. Whatever you need and are ready for will start seeping in or inspire you to experiment. Honor small steps that you choose to take. All feelings and emotions can be received and welcomed, but most of us have more trouble with some than with others.

Anger and fear are often among the difficult ones. Both are natural emotions and are likely to come up for cancer patients and veterans, perhaps more than in ordinary life. They are neither good nor bad, right nor wrong. They are a natural part of our human feelings—which doesn't mean we always welcome them easily! Because they may be unpleasant to experience or because of training or personality, some of us may be uncomfortable with either or both. Sometimes one emotion masks the other. Because of the nature of cancer, we may also find that the sheer intensity of these feelings threatens to overpower us.

There are a lot of theories about anger and disease: that blocking anger may cause disease, that getting in touch with or/and expressing anger is the royal road to recovery. My totally unexpert, unscientific *feeling* is that it may be *one* road, right for some people at some times— perhaps particularly suitable for someone who has stored unexamined anger over a long period and now feels ready to encounter it. Anger can be a route out of depression, releasing precious imprisoned energy. If these are issues for you, unlocking your anger, perhaps even with the safety of professional guidance, could be your road to recovery. But I doubt that it is the right or only way for everybody, and feeling that you have to approach healing from cancer through anger could add to the burden.

Because my family was uneasy with anger when I was a child, I now monitor myself for it and am concerned if I don't feel it when in a situation that I expect would set it off. In my family, my father sometimes looked grim, but expressing anger "wasn't done," certainly not "in front of the children." I rarely heard him say anything stronger than "Oh, pshaw," when irritated by misbehaving inanimate objects, never mind the ups and downs of human interaction. My mother, with standard female training, rather thought that if she felt anger it was a personal character flaw. It was a revelation to me that John and I could feel and express anger and not have it strike the marriage down as if by Jovian bolt. Anger and I have come a long way together since the time, years ago, when thinking about expressing it to my therapist caused me to get on the freeway headed in the opposite direction! Still, anger is not my easiest friend and I want to be sure I'm not squashing it. I want to be able to acknowledge it and choose how to relate to it, rather than be governed by it or try to escape from it.

Aware of the unhealthiness of repressed anger and the success stories of people who claimed their anger as the source of healing, I worried—especially at the beginning of my journey—that perhaps I was denying anger, because it wasn't surfacing as much as I might have expected. I was relieved when my psychiatrist-college roommate reflected that the onslaught of diagnosis and initial procedures was appropriately bringing out immediate survival responses more than anger. It may help you, as it did me, to be reminded that *we don't necessarily feel what we might expect or what others expect us to feel at any given moment.* I learned also to trust the timing of my feelings. When we are threatened by cancer, an inner wisdom may know when to hold back and when to give us full awareness of our feelings.

Here are excerpts from a journal piece I wrote when anger erupted at the very beginning of the cancer trail, and I felt completely and terrifyingly boxed in by my circumstances. I had had the mammogram, but nobody could make an educated guess whether what it showed was malignant. My surgeon had just explained the next steps and the unlikeliness of certitude, even if needle and surgical biopsies came back negative. I saw myself in a new and on-going, frightening life situation if cancer were not discovered. Yet I hardly wanted the certainty of a cancer diagnosis!

*   *   *

September 25

I am a storm of anger and I hardly know how to withstand my own turbulence. I am a terrified, raging, hissing, clawing, trapped animal. I am a volcano spewing molten lava over an entire landscape. I am a wrathful Zeus impatient with the petty problems of mere mortals. This is a whole new experience of anger.

Without sidestepping the anger I feel, I need also to stay where things are at this moment. I'm living out into the future. Stay with the present moment, Judy. Right now the worst of the bad is how my mind is torturing me. Since my mind is causing the disturbance, it can also offer the cure.

So, My Anger, I receive you. I accept you. As threatened as I am, both by what brings you on and by your violence, I'll do my best to befriend you. What I want in return is that you not spill onto other people or tag on to other situations, even though this upheaval aggravates and brings on other worries: about money; about my writing, which I am so afraid of having interrupted again; of being unable to listen and be with others in the way that is meaningful to me. So, we have a new task here, you and I: to find a partnership and respect for each other's needs. I want to affirm my faith in my processing ability and deep trust in who I am. It helped to give such big expression to my rage. I feel a tiny bit calmer, and now an image is forming.

My Anger, you make me feel like someone who was living a quiet, genteel life in the English countryside at the time of World War II, who suddenly had to open her home to Blitz evacuees from London. You are a boarder in my house now for an undetermined time. I admit I'm nervous about how we'll get along, because you are rowdier and more ill-mannered than my usual style. But there is a war on, and if I remember that you are here because of that, then we will learn how to set up housekeeping in a way that respects each other's needs. I want to be clear about our relationship to each other and to the things that set you going. We must be on the same side, and we will be if we communicate and clear tangles as soon as they happen.

*　　*　　*

As well as giving me significant relief from distress, the writing established an early relationship with my anger and made conscious my desire to work with it. I did other things in behalf of that relationship. I bought a styrofoam bat and ball for physical expression and release of anger. I didn't make much use of them, but knowing I had the resource was reassuring. For a spell after the end of treatment, when I felt disoriented and was left with the pieces of my life to pick up, I released anger—and dust!— by beating the sofa cushions with my vintage tennis racquet. I did it from a kneeling position to avoid strain to my back, and recalled tournament and team victories this old friend had won in college. Sometimes angry dance movement worked well for me. And, of course, anger did come out verbally at both appropriate and inappropriate times.

Some people are trained to feel that although anger is an acceptable emotion, fear is not. Some are afraid of experiencing their vulnerability. In such cases, anger can mask fear and vulnerability. The anger in the journal entry came on top of feeling terrified and trapped. Sometimes when we get angry and outraged at small annoyances—or at people connected with our treatment—it may be a way of avoiding our feelings of fear and vulnerability. If everything makes you angry, it might be worth daring to tap into the feelings of fear underneath. You may be surprised to find that comforting fear can also be empowering.

Getting acquainted with any feeling, or *how you relate to that feeling*, can help you become allies rather than enemies. If anything you want to investigate feels threatening, before you approach it, explore in writing what conditions would make it safe for you. *You* decide what are comfortable boundaries—how far you take your investigation at a given moment and in what manner. Here are some writing or musing suggestions that may help you:

Start by finding words, phrases, images, or short sentences that describe whatever you choose to shine your light on. It is okay not to like or approve of things you find out. Remember, if anything feels too big or overwhelming, you can start by finding the right distance between you and it.

As you write, notice if there is something impeding your having an open forum with yourself. Self-criticism? Embarrassment? Anxiety? Impatience? Drawing a blank? Something undefinable? Rather than trying to barge past interferences, see if you can name them as they come up. If naming it is enough to remove a barrier, you may want to go on. If it doesn't remove the barrier, see if you can just acknowledge the barrier in a friendly, accepting way. Perhaps you can even be a little curious about it without pushing or demanding anything of it or of yourself. If you gain new awareness just by naming and accepting the barrier, consider spending a little time with that new awareness. In both cases, taking time in this way may give you more than you imagine possible. For instance, taking as an example the anger expressed in the journal, let me show you another way I could have moved with it, one which might have been especially helpful had I run into a barrier of not accepting the anger.

Anger . . . afraid I'll be overwhelmed by it and just be angry all the time and that doesn't make me feel like me. Know it's meant to be good to feel my feelings, but I'm just afraid they'll overpower me. Feel bullied by some popular 'isms that "You're meant to be angry." Not comfortable with that either.

Hmm . . . Could I let all these feelings speak up and be accepted without having to resolve anything—the anger and the fear under-neath it, the fear I'll be overwhelmed by such intense anger, that I'm being bullied, and that the anger won't abate? Could I give each a piece of paper to write on until all the conflicting and threatened feelings are written down somewhere and then receive them all as my guests? My only job is to be a hostess who makes them feel welcome and understood.

Just receiving all the feelings in a kindly way may bring surprising relief, but feel free to do whatever might ease you a little further: talk gently to your feelings; let them talk to you; write or say affirmations; make an invitation of any kind, including one to some part of you that could help; write them a letter; create any kind of scene or environment that allows you to keep company with them. As you receive or validate, you can also include whatever helps you feel safe and protected or tells your side of the story. And remember that some form of physical move-ment may also help express and discharge distressingly intense feelings.

Here's to you and the rich world of all your emotions.

Love, Judy

March 3

Dear Friends,

Once home from the January bone marrow harvest followed by the third of six chemos, recovery is slower than after previous chemos. I do not spring back in twenty-four to forty-eight hours. This time, it's the better part of a week.

One day I feel really out of balance. I ask myself a question that helps when something is wrong and I haven't quite put my finger on it: "What's the worst of everything that's upsetting me right now?" The answer comes back that something is tampering with my self-esteem. That means my inner critic is at work, sending poisonous subliminal messages. I listen inside until the information comes. I've been losing my temper and getting angry at John. I have trouble accepting anger when it spews out over someone else, especially somebody who is doing so much for me. Yeah. I wish it weren't happening, and I've been trying to control it and still it happens again, and I haven't been liking myself as a result.

Okay. Much as I wish it were different, the first thing I need to do is fully accept and love myself, just as I am, Judy-who-is-spilling-anger-onto-John. I put an arm around that anger and let it know it is not a "bad guy." As I spend time with that awareness and let myself feel love for myself, my body lets go. I know I have touched the core of the problem. I am no longer at odds with myself. As a result, the anger shrinks, and now it is no problem to address the issues.

*   *   *

I regain my umph little by little and just begin to go out. I pulled my back out while in the hospital. Lying around is not good for it. I'm delighted that I can go to the chiropractor and start helping it. I'm on the brink of further mending when the nadir comes and with it, a respiratory infection. With its low white cell count, I know my body is susceptible, but it is a blow, nonetheless. I have a fever and a racking cough, which is also hard on my back. In spite of antibiotics, the infection goes on for more than a week, and just when I feel it should turn a corner, my fever goes up again. The doctor orders an X-ray. I have pneumonia. Aaargh! This feels like dirty pool, but now that we know it is pneumonia, other antibiotics will deal with fever and the worst of the cough in a few days. However, overall recovery and return of energy will take three to four weeks. Before the diagnosis, I was fighting my situation as I heard the clock ticking away my precious healthy time before the next chemo. Now I need to let go of that hope. At home, I grump loudly, then move toward changing my expectations.

A friend, who has been a nurse, comes to visit that evening. Her good listening and reflection help me toward making the necessary emotional shift. She speaks directly to the critic we know is lurking. "The medical profession has a word for your condition," she says. "You are immuno-depressed. It does not mean that if you could have done better, this wouldn't have happened." Several times she says, "You're sick," and I realize that in spite of it all, I haven't really accepted that. It's coming through now, and I'm beginning to stop fighting and relax. This pneumonia brings with it a major change in my perception of my situation. Up until now, I've had roughly predictable spells of normal energy between treatments, when I could widen my world by going out and seeing friends. Now I have to accept being shut in the house, mostly in bed, with low energy. Furthermore, there is no guarantee against similar things happening in the future. I begin the task of acceptance as we talk.

I pull out one other thread that is helpful. Getting pneumonia feels so punishing, yet I know it is impersonal, not somebody being nasty to me. But I am a person who relates very personally in the world. I hate the impersonal. Even though I know better with my head, I suddenly register that *for me, the impersonal feels like negative personal*. I feel myself relax after bringing all these things to awareness.

* * *

In spite of being mainly prone in bed, I can do the last steps of the letter I've worked on in bits and pieces through this time. Interspersed with rest, I can also do tiny tasks that give me satisfaction. I'm surprised how well I do emotionally, especially given the deprivation of people and the outside world.

One morning I have a dream that shows me my impatience with this limited life of tiny tasks. Someone wants me to help clean squid. I had to do that job once, and for my money, once in a lifetime is a heavy overdose of squid cleaning. In the dream, a friend tells me that I am belligerent. "Well," sez I, "I really would like to be useful, but I don't feel very well and this job with the squid, nope, I'm sorry, I'm just not going to do it." I explain that my belligerence is a product of trying to do when doing is too much.

I feel the need for something to cheer and lighten me—play, humor, color. I fantasize using crayons or paints, but the real activity seems too much work. What could I do right here in the house, not requiring umph, people, or landscape? I long for merriment. My, how I loved my fiftieth birthday party—eighty friends in a huge hall. I drift back to all the pleasures of that homey potluck and surprise dance band. What color, what sounds, what movement, what community! But I have relived that enough. I need something new, play freshly created in this moment.

My belly jiggles. Last night I watched British comedian John Cleese's sketch that takes place in the "Ministry of Silly Walks." Cleese, as bureaucrat, is questioning a client who seeks a grant to develop his silly walk. After the man demonstrates his walk, which alternates a long dipping stride with a jerky little hop, Cleese gets up and circles the room in an outrageous spaghetti-legged, whole-body stagger. Collected once again behind his desk, he intones platitudes about the difficulty of funding, and British to the core, rings for tea. It is brought in by a woman with a walk so jolting that the tea and all the crockery on the tray are in shambles by the time she sets it down. She lurches out with the smug expression of one who knows she does her job exquisitely.

So now I know what I want:

A Party of Silly Walks

Come, all of you who read these letters:
Doctors, nurses, friends, unknowns.
For just this moment, leave all purpose.
Selling, buying, teaching, study.
Changing diapers, scrubbing, fixing.
Healing patients' heads and bodies.
Playing music, writing, painting.
Tending money, books, and parks.
Making films, shampooing heads.
Baking, arguing in court.
Drawing plans and pulling weeds.
Pause from purpose, work, and business.
Let your mind go on a walk.

Choose your garbs: frock coats or tutus,
Skivvies, teagowns, buskins, caps.
Choose your colors: soft or jazzy,
Piebald, marbled, dotted, checked.
Rehearse your walk or be impulsive.
Parade or amble, shuffle, stride.
Shamble, hobble, toddle, slouch.
Careen or wriggle, scoot or bounce.
We'll have solos, duets, and trios.
Crowd scenes to rival MGM.
Mince or swagger, slink or sidle.
Quaver, falter, twitch, and reel.
Greet or snub another walker.
Blow a kiss or arch your brows.
Bump and wobble, hop and scramble.
Flitter, shudder, flap your arms.

An orchestra can match your movement,
Or go ahead: make up your sound.
Whistle, gurgle, chortle, chant.
Hiccup, snicker, wheeze, or pant.
Invent your body for this moment.

Invent a sound that isn't talk.
And when you've lived this other being,
Gently, when you've had enough,
Go back refreshed to purpose, business,
As I go on, relaxed to healing.
Healing after Silly Walks.

Digging up and spending time with so many deliciously foolish words gave me a project while lying in bed that entertained me over a good spell of time.

*   *   *

It is the nature of pneumonia that I don't notice gradual steady steps of improvement. It's more like living in a cocoon, knowing that eventually I will emerge into a different world, but for a longish span I just loll along in minimally differentiated time.

The week before I go back to the doctor, I am anxious and beset by images of dragging myself into chemotherapy a few days later. He listens to my lungs and says he wishes he had a medical student handy because I'm such a fine example of "coarse rales." I hear "rails."

"Well, no wonder there's such a ruckus of gurglings, bubblings, and poppings, if I have foul-mouthed marsh birds in my lungs." With my poor showing in the sciences in my schooldays, it makes me burst with pride to be constantly upgrading my medical knowledge now.

Due to illness, the February 20 chemo is canceled. I am grateful. I have another week, and then the doctor will see if I need yet another. I am so relieved that I ask John if we can stop for frozen yogurt on the way home. Once inside, I cough so excessively that I worry about the reaction of the clerk and other patrons. "It's okay," I reassure them. "It's not contagious. It's just pneumonia." I feel my distance from the ordinary world.

In addition to the challenge of how to entertain myself is an issue that I think affects most of us when we are sick, even with the flu. It is deep in our American values to be independent and productive. Illness puts us in conflict because we can't be. I've done remarkably well asking for and accepting help. I've been able to listen to friends in ways that are meaningful on both sides and keep me feeling connected. I've been able to satisfy my inner accomplisher with little tasks. But there are times when any activity is tantamount to cleaning squid. I need to shake down emotionally and physically to another level.

One morning I retrieve a dream about a cow, an energetic bull, and some frolicking calves in my backyard. I watch, fascinated, as the cow comes through a long passageway into my house. Then I worry whether the feisty bull and cavorting calves will also come in. The dream makes it clear that only the cow has access to this passage and the inside of my house. I lie in bed and receive that cow, for me the ultimate image of placid do-nothingness, knowing that the bull energy and the calf playfulness, which are also parts of me, will not intrude on what needs to be cow time. Through the day I conjure up that cow whenever some part of me considers pressing to do some little task.

Another day, I look outdoors and see cumulous clouds riding the hills and a few blossoms opening on the plum tree in our parking strip. For the first time, I feel my deprivation of the outdoor world. I think of country explorations I used to take some years ago. They haven't been a part of my recent life, but my yearning for them, like food when appetite returns, tells me I must be feeling better.

I go out and smell one of the few open flowers. It makes me cry for almond trees blossoming along some old haunt country roads. As I gaze at the clouds, I begin to travel in my imagination down an old friend of a back road that winds sixty miles through wild hills of Northern California. On my left, a creek gurgles. On my right, high walls of rock give way to steeply rising slopes sprinkled with blue oak, digger pine, and juniper. I cross a tiny bridge. The road winds up and out into the warmer, dryer air of hills covered with sage and manzanita. I lust for that landscape.

I've got it! I will dance to a Telemann flute fantasia tape I used to play in the car as I traveled that road. It is such magical, woodsy music that, on occasion, I even got out to dance, once in the light of a full moon. Even a minute or two will celebrate this tiny, precious, borning energy and give me more of that road.

I am met by a series of frustrations. There is no tape player in the house that will work. One does just long enough to tease me, then the batteries moan to a halt and I search for new ones, but can't get them to work either. I rage and vilify these haughty, defiant pieces of technology. Why must I be slapped down just when I think of one tiny spontaneous act that would give me pleasure? As I swear, alone and uncensored, an observing part of me says, "Ah, yes, remember that the impersonal means `nasty personal' to you?" Another observing part says, "That's more energy than you've had before. Even though you'd rather spend it dancing, look at that life force."

*   *   *

One day I feel the energy to return phone calls to friends who have left messages on the answering machine. I have an inspiring talk with a cousin long-distance. When I say that it is so weird to say "I have cancer and pneumonia," that I have to laugh at the preposterousness of it, she asks, "'Have' or 'had' cancer?" This takes us into a musing discussion which is very helpful.

Unlike the first cancer, I have not been able to assume this time that the cancer was out of my body right after surgery. But as I play with mental approaches, I think, Why not take a stance now that the cancer is ousted and that we do the rest to bar re-entry? It eases and lightens my mental state in two ways. First it allows me to let go of a vague background worrying into the future. I took a similar mental action in "deciding" that I would not have an experimental bone marrow transplant. I found that I was hanging onto the possibility of it in a harmful way. When the full information is available, I will have to look at it, but in the meantime I will no longer even consider the possibility. I will carry only the known program of chemotherapy and radiation. In the same way, I can change how I carry cancer in my awarensess. I go on doing my anti-cancer dance simply by continuing to center myself in each moment, by keeping my inner space as clear of clutter as possible, and then by doing whatever helps me through each treatment, each recovery, each difficulty.

The second way in which this attitude helps lighten my load is by preventing the occasionally recurring feeling that I ought to be doing something different, more specific, more often, or regularly to get rid of the cancer. For all my ability and enjoyment in working with hypnosis, dreams, and visualization, I have to watch out not to turn even these activities into tasks. For some people, routine—be it for healthy eating, exercise, visualization, spiritual practice, or alternative therapies—is a constructive way of contributing to the healing process. For me, who already engages in such things but in my own irregular way, routine risks adding a burden of "shoulds" which set off old inner alarms that I'm not doing enough or doing things right. My confidence and contribution to my healing are best when I can be creative, permissive, spontaneous, and playful. These qualities help keep my spirits positive and give me a sense that I am leading my life.

*   *   *

Another week has gone by. Before this doctor's appointment, I'm not burdened with images of dragging into chemotherapy, so I know I feel better. Though I would like another week's respite, it does not seem so overwhelming if I have to go.

Our February spring has arrived after uncharacteristic cold. For this outing I wear my new spring hat. A friend, whose creativity flows in behalf of my headgear, has presented me with a crocheted hat of blue and green mossy cottons. Into the "moss" she has anchored two plastic lizards. I sally forth into the world, a candidate for the Easter parade.

On seeing the lizards, my doctor recalls the Philippines, where a host of geckos lived on the ceiling of his house. He appreciated them because they ate other less charming household wildlife.

Today he has the letter I asked him to write to the insurance company, recommending the benefits of hypno- and psychotherapy for anxieties associated with cancer. I got such a "prescription" from my surgeon at the time of the last cancer and it resulted in the insurance company covering a major part of the professional psychological work I found helpful. I thank my oncologist for the wonderful and—I hope—convincing letter. "But," I add, "maybe to clinch the argument, you should just add 'And she arrives in my office wearing lizards on her head.'"

*　　*　　*

My lungs are better. The marsh birds have largely departed. I am grateful, though, that my doctor gives me another week, setting the fourth three-day hospital chemo for Monday, March 5. There isn't the same definitive end to pneumonia that there is to treatments, but my spells of energy are increasing. I am able to get to the chiropractor again to ease the damage to my back induced by coughing and inactivity and to strengthen it for the rigors of the coming chemo-induced inactivity. On the way to his office, I see a bumper sticker that delights me:

Wherever You Go, There You Are.

We are there with ourselves wherever we are, and we are wherever we are, whether we like it or not. It feels important both to be able to live wherever we are *and* to know how to help ourselves lessen the intensity of an adverse place. And finally, we do not always have the mobility to go either there or away, but . . . there we are.

Love, Judy

Dear Reader,

So many things can contribute to healing! I've talked a lot about being with your feelings and body in a friendly, supportive way. Equally important are laughter and pleasure. You doubtless already have favorite sources of enjoyment and draw from them as much as possible, but sometimes your access can be limited. Humor and play are by nature spontaneous, and it may be hard to know how to tap into that spontaneity when you're living with illness or too long stuck indoors. In this letter I want to offer you leads to some accessible forms of distraction, self-entertainment, humor, playfulness, and something I call sensory immediacy.

I was looking forward to writing to you about play and humor but instead, I've been in the grip of my curmudgeon critic. He grumbles that nothing is less humorous than writing *about* humor. His folded-arms, lean-away stance says, "I'm not going to cooperate." So right now I'm going to turn my back on him and engage in one of the techniques I want to offer to you: *nonsense writing*—moving my pencil steadily for about ten minutes, letting my static-filled, resistant mind be jostled, jogged, jiggled, and juicified.

*   *   *

The fluidity found fatuous fears in furballs forced out of elevator doors. Mary rode a turkey to Turkey and offered it for a mascot, while

*frying potatoes in her swimming pool and the gnats sang Christmas
carols over the counter. Did the oldest gnat win a gold watch for all
those years of service or just some grumplepoppy jelly beans in the
shape of palm trees and spiffy, spanking spatulas, touring Europe in a
cattle car, fitted out with wheezing werewolves wearing gold chains,
not only around their necks, but also as ankle bracelets, each
werewolf trying to outdo the other, waffling as the breezes blew,
threw, phew, pew, porous pots parading eternally in and out of whisk-
brooms, roaring up the windpipe of the storm across tropical oceans,
forty inches long and three-sixteenths of an inch wide with no measur-
able height, except for one mermaid rising out of the pink sea, wearing army boots for earrings.*

* * *

There. You see? My critic unbent and got drawn into play. I feel a lot
better and I hope you get the idea. Nonsense writing is generally gramm-
atical; that is, it has subjects and verbs, adjectives modifying nouns, and
so forth. But, of course, you can do whatever suits you—strings of adjectives, rhyming words, etc. I often let sentences go on and on, one clause
emerging from another in an endless flow that increases free association. I
may get into an eddy of words based on sound, and sometimes throw in
made-up words. As incongruous images emerge, your brain will gradually
get drawn into the foolish fun of it, or the footish fumes of it, or the furry

foam of it. It is good not only for loosening up the stuck-'n-stale writer, but also for any mind gone creaky and dour. You may also let nonsense lead you into a real subject, which you can now approach with let-'er-rip abandon. I suspect you might loosen up similarly by singing nonsense or talking nonsense into a tape recorder, in a round-robin group or with a friend, or while moving or dancing. I don't generally recommend talking nonsense to your doctor—well, probably not on your first appointment.

Here are a few other writing suggestions to elicit your humor.

1) Describe how something looks or is experienced by an outsider—someone from a different culture, planet, or any other point of view. For instance, how might an extraterrestrial or someone from the seventeenth century react on walking into one of our high-tech hospitals?

2) Choose someone or something that bugs you or a situation that was not funny at the time, like having your front door bang and lock shut when you were outside in bathrobe and slippers, picking up the newspaper. Try stepping back from your real feeling or usual point of view about it. Just describe it by heaping up all its preposterous details.

3) Imagine a sober person or solemn situation, suddenly intruded on by something or someone that blows its/his/her ability to perform—react—happen as usual. For example, the staff-meeting windbag is suddenly interrupted by the entrance of a man sporting a wizard hat, pedalling into the room on a unicycle, announcing that he's from the cleaning agency

and was told to start in this room.

4) Imagine yourself dressed in some uncharacteristic way or in an uncharacteristic situation and describe it. Perhaps you're earning a few extra bucks doing a promo job downtown that requires you to wear a giant chicken costume. Your oncologist appears, and you say something sociable in your best barnyard voice, like, "Adriamycin comes from the Adriatic. Here's a coupon to chow down at 'Clucky Wucky's!'"

5) Take any two incongruous things—people, person and place or situation, place and situation, person and thing—and see what happens as you describe them. For example, imagine a prima donna-like person you know stranded in the wilderness or yourself stumbling onto an outdoor movie set thinking it was a real restaurant, as I once did in Italy.

And here's an offering for those times when you need minimal-effort entertainment without the noise of television or videos: cartoon books can be a great resource. I found the big, colorful pictures, large print, and brief dialogue were just about my speed when I was in my three-day chemo stints.

Sensory Immediacy

When ill and in the hospital, we often have unpleasant sensory experiences. Making a point of attending to positive ones helps counteract the nasties. We also can experience sensory deprivation when we're too long shut in the house, hospital, and medical buildings. Even in ordinary life, we tend to rush along, focused on the list in our heads, forgetting to take nourishment from the sensory pleasures of our surroundings.

One of the compensations of being limited is that you may begin to notice and take pleasure in little moments, little physical details: the wind blowing a tree outside a window, the way the sun forms a patch on the floor and wall and how it moves and changes shape, a bird on a feeder placed outside a window, a spider scuttling up an invisible web, the texture and color of curtains you've lived with for years.

Some hospitals have an art cart that comes around. Getting a picture on the wall can help enormously. Bone marrow transplant rooms are sterile and don't allow plant material, but the ones I occupied (because they were the only much-desired private rooms available) had bulletin boards. Even a calendar picture tacked up helps. Once, I deliberately wore to the hospital a pink t-shirt decorated with butterflies that a friend had just given me. When I put on my johnnie, I tacked the t-shirt on the bulletin board for my three-day stint.

Drop into your own rich storehouse of recollections. You can retake a trip or resavor humorous, restful, or meaningful events. When you're physically able, playing with colored pencils, crayons, rubber stamps, playdough, or paint can also help counteract sensory sterility. Looking at or reading children's books may offer the senses some pleasure, put you in touch with hopeful feelings, and give you time away from the complexities of illness and adult life.

Here are some writing (or imagine-in-your-head if you have to lie in bed) suggestions that can give you sensory immediacy of a pleasant nature when your surroundings don't offer any.

You can describe in as much detail as possible any of the following: an object, a place, a person, an animal, a fleeting moment, a scene of action or interaction. Any of these can be real or imagined or a combination. Try to include as many of the five senses as possible or experiment with one of the senses you might not ordinarily think to describe.

When you are in waiting, treatment, or hospital rooms, delight in the auditory tidbits people share with you:

"I was brought up in a town with two traffic lights. I could get lost in a paper bag."

"I had a relationship with my refrigerator. I was in the spotlight as soon as I opened the door."

"I haven't had the world's most successful marital life: I've discarded husbands at the rate others discard running shoes."

Eavesdrop on conversations. Sometimes the best are only partially heard:

"Betsy's ____?____ is, but Betsy's mother's brother's wife isn't."

Enjoy accents: "I have to wash my flaws today." (Rhode Island for "floors.")

If you're being driven to the hospital, doctor's office, or home, or are suffering from reiterating logistics in your head as you run errands, let your

118

eyes take in what's out there. Revel in the kid bicycling along, followed by two dogs wearing t-shirts. Delight in the cat drinking from a dripping sprinkler.

Enjoy foolish signs: "Fight mouthwash. Eat garlic."

When I'm not wearing my glasses, signs sometimes provide interest beyond the author's intent. My mind was once jarred to attention by a bulletin board notice that read: "Sex without classes." A closer look revealed: "See without glasses." Well, I do, I do. A whole world of wonder and foolishness is there to greet us when we open the door.

I hoped I've pushed it ajar for you.

Love, Judy

April 25

Dear Friends,

   The fourth (early March) and fifth (early April) chemos go unbelievably better than the third. Since the fifth, my continuing psychological journey and robust health, allowing for normal life out in the world, have given happy competition to completing this letter.

*   *   *

   A few days after my return from the fourth chemo, I share my inner explorations with a visiting friend. I am concerned that I'm not engaging more in imagery work to fight cancer. "There is something uncomfortable about that for me. How do I confront this impersonal, cellular thing in my body that I can neither see nor feel? It could be personalized as an enemy or an unwitting but dangerous intruder, but still I can't engage."

   My friend's response surprises me and shifts my awareness to an unexpected part of my questioning. "You're not a confrontational person," she says. This sets us both recalling examples of how I've handled conflicts with people. I do not go head-on, and my way is generally more effective than head-on would be. Though cancer is not another person with feelings that need to be respected, I feel this bit of insight puts me on the right track. Whatever my approach toward cancer, it needs to be compatible with my basic personality. In some sense that I don't yet understand, my fighting cancer doesn't have to be "head-on."

I find myself talking about how much I want to live, how much I want to continue the writing I am doing and get it out there to share with others, and how much gusto I've been feeling in the process. I want to feel that because I have such a strong sense of purpose, surely that will make me healthy, make me live. Yet I know that people have been cut down in mid-work. There's no guarantee. Then I realize I don't know anything about what was going on inside those people. That's different from what I know about myself—the power, confidence, and purpose that have been developing.

Suddenly, from all the things we've been tossing around, a powerful feeling accompanied by a phrase pops to the surface. "I feel a *deep willing* to heal, a *deep willing* to live." In the usual action-oriented American tradition, spurred on by my worried critic and doer, I've been assuming that "fighting cancer" is a matter of actions, of fight-back visualizations. But this phrase *deep willing* fills me up and resounds with meaning. *My whole being* feels engaged. . . . Oh. . . . So *this* is what is meant by that cliché, "the will to live."

Over the next week I have several experiences of touching those intense feelings accompanied by more insight. I'm still not at ease with the fact that I don't engage in visualization to fight cancer. A medical friend points out that visualization is just one tool for mobilizing the body's healing systems. Another important aspect of healing is living in and enhancing the healthy part. "I've noticed that you live largely out of the non-cancer part of yourself. You've had no problem of depression. Your personality is intact. The very way that you live and your own range of approaches are probably already activating your body's healing systems."

Alone, on another occasion, I quietly consider the question, "What's to lose by an all-out belief in my healing?" Of course the catch is, Would I feel like a failure if there were a recurrence of the disease?

As I stay quietly in the presence of this issue, it comes intuitively that this has *nothing to do with success and failure*. There is a lot of mystery in this business of illness and healing. None of us really knows what we can affect and what is outside our realm. For me, it is important not to get into a "trying-hard," "working-hard" mode. I notice that earlier I wrote "imagery work." When imagery comes spontaneously out of my needs or interest, it doesn't seem like work. If I think I must sit down and do it on command, it feels onerous, and I resist the imposition.

Visualization is not a task. Healing is not a task. It is a way of being toward myself, toward life, toward the unknown. All day I let that awareness and the sentence *Failure is not an issue here* accompany me.

* * *

A few days later I drive for the first time in five or six weeks. I set a modest goal of a nearby library with the option to continue to the park. Wowie! Driving is delicious! I sail past the library, through and out the other side of the park. The car winds and dips and climbs the rolling hills. This road is an old friend and today is as fresh as new love. Horses graze along the way. Cattle browsing high up on a sheer hill form a daring vertical line of brown against the green. Almond trees and yellow mustard flowers are abloom. Buckeye trees have just put forth their tender, handlike leaves. Thirty minutes later I enter another park, where the road narrows and rises until I look down over the expanse of valley below and across to Mt. Diablo. I even take a fifteen minute walk and greet yellow fiddlenecks—my first wildflowers this season. Oh, the triumph of freedom! The triumph of spring!

*　　*　　*

One morning before I am fully functional, I thoughtlessly lean over to pick up a piece of paper off the floor, and my back goes into painful spasms. Aaargh. Ouch. And a string of four-letter words. My back rarely goes into spasm since long-term chiropractic treatment, but it is more vulnerable from long inactivity, and now the adjustment to activity. It responds well to muscle relaxants, ice packs, and two good nights' sleep. But then it goes into spasm again. This really upsets me because one of my sisters is due to arrive that night. We've arranged for her to come after the nadir is over, when my energy is good again. In spite of my back trouble, I was mending well enough that I thought we could still have a good visit. Now that feels threatened. *I* feel threatened. I go back to bed and drop into a deep encounter with the distress in my back and emotions. I listen inside myself in a kindly, acceptant way. I wait for information from my body. As I attend to the undefined feeling about all this, the words *discouraged* and *vulnerable* come. I can sense there's more there. Regret. Frustration not to be as fit as I would wish. Yes, and still something more than regret and frustration. Something about needing to be fit. It's more like . . . *my vulnerability feels endangering.* That's it. I get a distinct letting go in my body that tells me I've got new and significant information. And now the whole understanding that I need tumbles into full awareness.

When I was a child, certain feelings were not accepted in my family, and the child in me still remembers being attacked when vulnerable. So, now if a member of my family is coming when I feel vulnerable, of course the child in me feels endangered. As I lie there, I imagine myself putting an arm around that child and reassuring her that I, as an adult, will honor her vulnerability. I remind myself that my sister and I are adults who care for each other and no longer live in our original circumstances. Still I'm not sure how I would fare if she were to attack my vulnerability now, or even if she were not acceptant of it. I feel my way in further and wonder if that's a projection of some piece of me that might still attack my own vulnerability. I can't do anything about any other person's relationship to vulnerability—or whether they might attack mine because they don't accept their own—but I can, indeed, go deeper right now in accepting my own.

I hang out lovingly with the worried child, with my new awareness, and with my back, which needs me to give it the most relaxing, acceptant environment to heal in. Now I consciously breathe in a way that will help my back and the child relax. My sense of danger ebbs away. Even my feeling of vulnerability shrinks as I fill up with well-being and a new confidence that my back will not be long in getting better now. I drift off into a long sleep.

The next day, although my back is by no means perfect, I have a wonderful visit with my sister—the best I've ever had. I tell her what happened before she came. Lightly we range over childhood experiences and feelings with each other and in our family, as well as those that are important in our present lives. We laugh a lot and delight in the day.

*   *   *

The worried critic has been loitering on my property again. I became suspicious that he was present after I dreamed of trying to contain feisty dogs who had gotten loose (dogs are my dream symbol of the spontaneous, instinctual life); when I chased out a young woman who had entered my unlocked front door (surely some part of me I wanted to let in since I left the door unlocked); when, simultaneously, one under each hand, I subdued two cats by clutching the back of their necks and holding them down to the floor (cats are my dream symbol of love and affection). The dreams suggest to me that my critic is constricting and stifling me with subliminal messages. I've learned that he does that when he's anxious.

"So, my nervous, need-to-be-doing friend, come on out of the shrubbery and let's talk things over. Sit down on the lawn with me and tell me what's worrying you."

"This thing you're trying to do, this vague connecting with deeper healing powers. I don't think you're doing it right, and I don't know how to do it."

"That's right. You don't. But it's not your responsibility. Leave it to me. I have found over and over in the last decade that when I remember that I have everything I need within me, I don't have to know how. The 'how' comes on its own. It may direct me toward a specific doing, but more often it comes as a shift in perception or a spiritual 'hit.' The 'how' is a continual series of little discoveries that can be named only after their emergence. Do you feel better that you don't have to take charge here?"

"Yes, I do. But . . ."

"There's more on your mind, isn't there?"

"Yeah. I'm really upset about those books you have about fighting cancer. The very first one you started to read just confirmed my feeling that you're not doing things right. You should be . . ."

"Whoa, there. You're right. I opened the first book and you laid into me. So I shut it, knowing that anything that got you that stirred up could not benefit my healing. I know what happened. The author felt she fit the definitions of 'the cancer-prone personality,' and she set to work to make deep changes in her personality and life. You and I lost our boundaries. We forgot that I am a separate person, and it triggered your fear that, after all, we must work and 'fix Judy.' Even the concept of a 'cancer-prone personality' set an alarm going!

"But I have an idea. Why don't you settle into that comfy lawn chair with a cup of tea, while I look at the book alone . . .

"Well, that cancer patient assessed her needs with courage and brought about astounding physical and psychological healing, but her situation and personality were different from mine. Perhaps some things could apply to me. But I think this book could again get you stuck in the question 'Did some emotional issue bring on this cancer?' and set you to desperate blaming, because you think I ought to be able to master everything! I know your deep-down worry: if I can't change some emotional issue that may have led to cancer, it could leave me wide open to more cancer. But that idea leads to panic, and we don't even know that an emotional issue led to these cancers. Another part of me knows this: For all that we can change, we can't change everything, and change is most likely to come through a trust-ful opening, not by trying to figure out causes or by fixing Judy. The view that if we change, we will be free of cancer appeals to you be-cause you want control. Sometimes it takes subtle learning to distinguish between taking an active stance and believing that we can control everything. I appreciate your desire to control things in order to protect me, but you can trust me to be in charge. When you're relaxed, another part of me is good at knowing when a book, a person, an activity, or an approach will contribute to my healing. Thanks for coming out of the shrubbery. I like the way you yawned and stretched out your legs just now."

*　　*　　*

The day after writing to my critic, I go for my first session of Trager Bodywork. It is deeply relaxing, a real gift to my beleaguered body, and it takes me to a centered place. (It's a good example of knowing that a person and a healing activity are right for me.) I come home and open another book I've been meaning to peruse, Stephen Levine's *Healing into Life and Death*. I find several things that speak to me: a "Don't Know" stance, a responsibility "to" rather than "for" your illness, the individual path of each patient, a man who poured love and forgiveness into his tumor, which shrank—a notion that appeals to me more than "fighting cancer."

That night I have a long series of dreams I have no trouble remembering, and I feel their power even before I unfold their meanings. Two dreams are particularly rich:

Dream #1: I want to swim in a pond I can see, but when I go to get in, it is covered with sand, and though I can see a man swimming underwater, I can't see how to get in. I walk around to another part, a sort of backside of the pond, and there the water is accessible, though it looks murky and scary. Suddenly, I'm aware there are animals in it, and one emerges straight up out of the water. In horror, I see it is an alligator and am grateful I saw it before entering the water. But as it rises from the water, it transforms into a creature that I refer to as a hippo, but which is in fact an almost bestiary, mythic combination animal with overtones of "horseness." Awake, this image excites me enormously.

Soon after the discovery of the first cancer, I had a dream of an alligator I was trying to get rid of, which was clearly a symbol of the cancer. Here it arises out of the waters of the unconscious, and in the process, transforms into a creature with aspects of hippo, which, from other associations, I take to be a calm, solid beingness rather than doingness. It is combined with the "horseness" of my creative energy. Horses are usually allied to my writing, which now has become a tool for my healing process, which, in turn, also requires creativity. The dream is spiritually powerful.

Dream #2: I visit a place called Lover's Leap, a waterfall. If one dares to jump over it, I understand she will land in the curative waters of the pool below. I do. Going through the air is a slow, almost motionless descent during which I have a fearless awareness of my leap. Then I'm in

the water, which gradually recedes until there is none at all, and I am standing, unscathed, with both feet fully planted on a brown (my dream color of self-identity) ground. Another numinous dream.

*   *   *

A couple of days later, I share all this material with the woman with whom I do hypnotherapy. She asks if I want to get in the water with the cancer on a hypnotic voyage. I'm both excited and scared. To make it safer, I take a number of meaningful figures into the water with me, including the underwater swimmer. On the bank, I place a giggling and delighted Daphne—the survivor child I was. She holds a rope that is fastened around my waist, in case things become too dangerous and I want to be pulled out of the water.

I spend an extraordinary explorative time, enriching the vitality of all the dream images and making further connections. The therapist asks when I became unprotected in a way that allowed the cancer to take hold. As she names different ages, I begin to feel threatened. It's partly because I've never been successful with that hypnotic technique, and my critic is engaging. But along with that comes a turbulence that sometimes indicates that I'm close to touching something painful. Spontaneously I call out, "I've always been unprotected—right from the beginning." I'm losing the trance now and feel myself up against a wall. We both invite me to just stay there at the wall, neither trying to find a way around it nor running away. That acceptance opens up a rush of experiences.

I feel grief for the person who could not protect herself from this cancer. I feel grief and love for the pneumonia-infested infant, Daphne, whose doctors, fearing that ordinary baby movement would endanger her, bound her to reduce motion. I cry as I recount my mother's hating this and being grateful to a night nurse who unbound and cuddled me. But in spite of that, I probably did not get all the cuddling love that would otherwise be offered a new baby. Now as I feel my grief, I give my love to this adult and that baby, and I glory in my powers of survival.

The rush goes on. I leap to a crucial part of the origins of the Worried Try-Hard, Never-Enough part of me. My mother was deeply unhappy in her marriage. My role was to make things better for her. But, of course, no matter how hard I tried, it was never enough. I see how these cancers—especially this one—could trigger the Try-Hard, Never-Enough in me. Haven't I done extensive and wonderful psychological work? Haven't I come through enormous midlife traumas and losses in a way that built new strength and understanding and joy of living? Don't I live a physically and emotionally healthy life? Then how could this !@#$%&* cancer—even nastier than the first one—develop? The crucial word—the crucial feeling—surges up. *Shame.* Of course. Shame I couldn't prevent this cancer with the same quality of the child ashamed she couldn't make things all right for her mother.

The grief. The shame. The full experiencing. The big release.

That night I dream of an enormous house with many people gathered at a party. I discover this house has whole apartments of living quarters I didn't know existed, and running carefree on busy childish adventure down a path outside is a little girl in a party dress the color of my healing green, accompanied by a spunky little dog.

Awake, I stand in awe of the human psyche.

My healing will go deeper.

Love, Judy

Dear Reader,

In the letter you just read, I had an extended conversation with my inner critic. This letter is devoted to the subject of the inner critic, because I suspect most people get some flak from it. The amount and nature of it can vary from minor skirmishes to attacks that can be extremely debilitating. Learning to recognize and deal with our inner critic can be important in ordinary life and crucial in times of crisis, such as cancer treatment. An overactive critic can rob precious energy we need for healing and, if extreme, can cause depression which, if extended, can work against healing.

I use *inner critic* because the term is perhaps the most easily understood, the least technical, and least attached to a particular school of psychology, and one that allows you to sketch in what fits for you.

These days many people are aware of their inner critic, but if you have not yet formed a relationship with yours, you may not know how to distinguish it from a serviceable part of you that helps you assess situations, make judgments, seek solutions, and correct errors. The crucial difference is that the critic is mean, shaming, punishing, attacking, denigrating. It's the voice that uses a lot of "nevers," "alwayses," and "should haves." It's inclined to be less interested in solving the problem than in laying blame. It's the voice that says you don't know what you're doing, you're not doing it right, and even that it's somehow your fault that you got cancer! Your critic may not be as extreme as that and may use subtler language. Learning to identify both its presence and its style can be most useful. My critic sometimes has valid points, but it doesn't offer helpful suggestions or solutions, and it rather enjoys sounding drastic! Some people find the critical tone is woven in with legitimate aid. Beware if your critic tells you it's treating you roughly for your own good, to help keep you in line. This argument is as specious as the one that justifies beating a child for its own good. There are more humane and more effective ways for all of us to learn what we need to know.

By getting acquainted with your inner critic, you can befriend it and undercut its misdirected power. As it becomes more concrete and visible, it becomes less slippery. The following exercises come from one of my writing groups for cancer patients. Toward the end of the first meeting, I asked if people wanted to continue with their own explorations or stop and share any of what they'd been writing. One woman said, "I'd just like to finish my paragraph, and then I'd like to stop and share." Another woman said, "Paragraph? Paragraph? I just have bits and pieces." Catching her anguished tone, I asked, "And is your inner critic unhappy about that?" "Oh, yes, it is," she answered, looking grateful that she had an ally. Her "bits and pieces" were not only a very useful investigation for her, but deeply moving and meaningful to the rest of us. So much for the trustworthiness of the critic's assessments.

These exercises are especially suited to writing, but for heaven's sake, please remember this is not an assignment! You may not want to write at all, but if you do, keep in mind that bits and pieces, lists, or notes are as legitimate as paragraphs! You may also adapt these suggestions to other activities: musing aloud or in your head, taking turns with a friend to discuss your critics or do an exercise aloud, drawing, playdough modeling, dancing, or acting your critic—alone or with a friend.

Describing the Critic

  * Is it male or female? Age or stage of life?
  * Does it make you think of a person in a certain kind of job, such as a bureaucrat who is overly focused on the importance of filling out forms correctly?
  * Does it remind you of a person from your childhood or present life—a scolding parent, a taunting older sibling, a strict teacher, a demanding boss, a neighborhood bully?
  * What kind of language does it use?—vocabulary, frequently repeated phrases, tones of voice? You can even record, as if by dictation, its statements.
  * What kind of gestures or facial expressions do you see?
  * How does it dress? How does it move?
  * Who does it want to be accepted by or impress?

Sometimes this exercise can give you helpful information. My critic is sometimes still a schoolchild casting others as teachers for whom it wants to perform well.

Addressing the Critic or Engaging in Dialogue

1) If your critic is really tyrannizing you, you may need to do most of the talking. You may need to *let it know you are in charge*. You may even need to tell it off in no uncertain terms, play the disciplinarian, or match its peevishness with your anger. This can bring your energy up to reclaim the space its energy has encroached on. Early in my relationship with my critic, I once shouted out loud and at length in sheer exasperation, and to my surprise, it disappeared like a street bully who has been faced down.

2) *Gentler, inquiring approaches* often work even better. You may want to invite it to state its complaints and worries, or why it feels obliged to harangue you. Sometimes my inner critic is a pained or anxious part of me that hasn't felt heard and accepted. It attacks because I've been ignoring legitimate needs, and it doesn't know how else to get my attention. Remember that to listen caringly is very different from believing its criticism or supporting its style. You may find that it speaks less abusively once you invite it to speak.

3) You may want to *investigate the critic's origins* in yourself. You might discover that it was astute at protecting you when you were a child.

For instance, if you were taught never, ever, to be late and were punished for minor tardiness, you may get a lot of flak from your critic if you are even a little bit or unavoidably late. Or you may find yourself being late out of unconscious rebellion and then getting attacked by your critic. If something like that is the case, your critic may still be acting as though the circumstances that brought it into being are the same. You may want to tell it what the present circumstances are and how they differ from when you were little.

4) If the critic sees itself as acting to protect you, you may wish to *express appreciation for its concern and desire to look after you*, and let it know that you have better ideas about how to do that. Usually the critic is more limited in its skills, imagination, and understanding of the world than you, as an adult, are.

5) You may need to *talk to the critic the way you would to a child* who has a legitimate gripe about a sibling or playmate, but is using violent or denigrating behavior. For example: "I know you're upset with me because you think I'm not spending enough time with _____ (my daughter, partner, family, work). I share your value, but right now it is even more important for me to get enough rest and get well. And I need you to work with me, not against me, and treat me with respect and understanding kindness."

6) Often if the critic feels heard, it will quiet down and be more receptive to your requests or directives. You can *ask it to sit at a dis-*

tance or go outside while you are not feeling well, or for a certain event or length of time.

7) *The critic may have some positive characteristics* and abilities that serve you well in some situations or if presented non-punitively. You may want to list its assets and let it know you appreciate them, and that you will give it an opportunity to exercise its skills at a later time or in another context. I see my critic in its positive form as my capacity for hard work, organization, and practical tasks. When it feels frustrated because I'm sick and can't let it perform in those ways, I like to let it know that I appreciate its abilities and that I will give it a chance to exercise them as soon as possible or in some smaller way.

8) You may wish to *enter into an equal dialogue* in which you and the critic each express your feelings about a given issue and your respective needs, *without any pressure to resolve differences*. It would be an occasion for both of you to fully express, listen, and be heard. You may be surprised to find something easing within you or even changing on its own when you do not seek solutions as part of your dialogue.

9) You may want to *ask the critic what it needs or wants from you*. It's important for you to know that you don't have to provide what it wants. Just as with a child who wants a pony, you can honor the critic's desires, without expecting yourself to provide. You can even agree with the critic about how nice it would be to have the things it wants or to be the way it would like you to be.

As with a child, your critic may respond better for having its want validated than if it is told, "You don't want that" or "That's foolish and unrealistic." Instead, you could say something like: "It *would* be really nice if I could do all the things I usually do, but for a while it is not advisable even to try." The same is true in reverse if the critic is attempting to convince *you* that you don't want something or it's foolish and unrealistic. In a sense, you are modeling behavior for the critic, teaching it gentler ways.

You may learn something unexpected, surprising, or useful when you ask the critic what it wants. You may even find that there is something you reasonably can offer it.

10) If you choose to do most of the talking, you may find that you *develop a tone* that quiets the critic and helps you to hear your own voice and strength. You can even deliberately use *hypnotic phrases and repetitions*. The phrase "more and more" can be useful, as in "I see you are becoming more and more relaxed, more and more trusting of my judgment about this."

Don't be shy about repeating yourself, even though repetitions can seem simple-minded. *Repetition in writing often helps the material to sink in therapeutically*. Repetitions with slight variations can have two useful effects: They can create calm because they speak to a primitive part of the brain, and they can help you find your more exact meanings.

11) You can *role play and pretend you are the critic*, writing its lines in as complete and even exaggerated form as possible. Sometimes if you carry it to the point of caricature, you tip over into humor. *Humor* almost always defuses the critic.

12) You can *describe your critic to yourself or another person*, which may bring on a sort of winking knowingness or recognition of the preposterousness of its attitudes or demands.

At different times different approaches work; what works well one time may not be the most effective the next. The act of creating a new approach in the moment can free you from submission to the critic and facilitate a breakthrough.

In summary, I think the most important thing you can do is whatever gets the critic to come out and face you, so that it doesn't engage in sneaky attacks from the rear. Another way to look at it is that you are casting light into the shadow where the critic lives. As you do, you are building a new relationship with it.

Here's to that deepening relationship.

Love, Judy

June 12

Dear Friends,

This letter covers the month before the sixth and final chemo, which takes place from Friday, May 3, to Monday, May 6. I find so much material in my journal for this time that I have decided to offer you mostly experiences relating to one important emotion: fear.

From knowledge of my past patterns, I am not surprised that fear comes to lurk more toward the end of chemo. When the crisis first hit, I experienced shock and adrenaline stepped up. Though I have lived with underlying fear and bouts of fear, I haven't been living with a continuous awareness of it. Rather, it transformed into devising creative routes through what I needed to get through. But when the onslaught of events begins to let up and the end of treatment is in sight, I have more leisure to be afraid of the future. The underlying worries, Is cancer licked? and Will it return? have room to move in. The scariest times can come when I'm not doing something on behalf of healing.

*   *   *

I've been wanting to try meditation, but I anticipate its arousing my inner critic, so I go for another hypnotherapy session to encounter my anxiety about being with stillness. I'm invited to attend to my breathing and, in particular, to the momentary empty spaces that occur naturally at the beginning and end of each breath. As I move into a place of increasing stillness, I experience the void in a frightening way. It is the dark of when I was a child alone in my room before falling asleep. I recall an era of musing on death at that young age, terrified of not existing. Hmm. Some of that childhood fear related to family matters. I recall another feature of that little girl nighttime. I was fascinated by the succession of tiny dots of light I saw in the dark, especially if my eyes were closed. I called them "prayers," because the word sounded to me the way the parade of tiny lights looked, and when I focused on them, I sensed a presence in the darkness.

I move on into the void that comes with being in stillness as an adult. It, too, is associated with death, with non-being—a great nothingness. It is the very opposite of color, life, love. But as I am with these meanings, and go on to consider the void as the place where life begins, something shifts. I get a new, positive experience of the void, one that pulsates with being. "A great nothingness" has shifted to "a great somethingness." I pay attention to that feeling so that I can really get its flavor. I hold the experiences of both the child and the adult, of both the great nothingness and the great somethingness. Opposites dissolve and the *voidsilencedark* becomes less threatening. I go back to the child's "prayers," those dots of light created by and seen only in the dark. I end by taking some time to just slosh around in the great somethingness. I have taken a step into the void and encountered some of its meanings. I have reduced fear just a little bit, even of death.

*　　*　　*

A few nights later I dream of a large, ample woman who observes me and comments on what she sees. Awake, I understand that a new and important dream figure has shown me an already "ample" part of myself who can help me as I risk the critic to try meditation. She is the uncritical, objective observer, the one who can note the presence of head chatter and encourage me gently to let it go.

*   *   *

In the next week I continue to experience fear on and off. One evening I ask John if he will just sit and accompany me and listen while I talk about my fears. I'm having an assault of resenting and fearing my illness and my uncertain future.

This evening John is the perfect listener, giving himself fully to just being with me, periodically reflecting what I say, but never interfering with suggestions, *never trying to get me to move beyond the fear*. Much of the time most of us don't listen in a way that is truly helpful when someone needs to talk about negative feelings. Because we feel the other person's distress and want to help alleviate it, we tend to offer suggestions or the bright side, and sometimes anything to stem the tide simply because it is difficult to hear. In my experience, it is not helpful to have the listener offer advice or a view of optimism or encouragement or help us to see the good side. It is certainly not helpful to point out that things could be worse or that other people have it worse or that we'd do better not to think about it. Fully receiving my own feelings and, in some instances, being heard and received by another caring person allows the feelings to shift on their own. It takes willingness and self-control on the part of the listener and trust that making the person feel truly heard can make a difference. As a result of John's full, empathic listening, my fear and resentment ebb. I relax and feel myself back in a normal relationship to my life.

Another theme running through this time is dreams containing green, my color of healing. The most cohesive and satisfying one is of being in a theatre. I have chosen a seat on the left side near the front, where I have room to spread out because there are no other people immediately around me. But the angle is such that I can't see a significant part of the stage action, so I move around the dark theatre, trying out different seats. I find the back row empty and choose a center seat behind a child so I can see the stage well. Just then the parents move in front of me and I need to shift seats again in order to have a full view of the action on stage. I start relating to the mother who, having just come in, wants to be told what has happened so far. I tell her that a big battle is being fought. I assure her that this is no violent TV-style shoot-'em-up; rather, colorful mythological figures in elaborate costumes, reminiscent of dragons and people in a Chinese New Year's Parade, are engaging in meaningful action. My attention focuses on the rich green in all the costumes and, in particular, on an eight-foot-tall and proportionately wide warrior, whose all-green costume and headgear flutter with long fabric ribbons. We are watching a drama of metaphysical dimensions, and I reassure the mother that it is suitable for both her and her child.

I have found the right place in the theater from which to see the whole play, and especially the almost-stylized dance actions of this larger-than-life, green-clad, mythological figure. I have also educated the mother to include the child, and made it possible for all of us to view this play together.

*   *   *

Another morning I wake and feel caught in fear again. It's a vague, generalized fear. I range over my dreams to see if something in them brought it up. The only one I clearly remember is of being in water, swimming around. I feel I should be able to take heart from that, as I've had a series of dreams in which I wanted to get in the water but was afraid to—and here now I've done it. Something is resolving. But right now that doesn't matter. My fear is so present, so great, so general, it seems to include everything ahead of me. I let myself be quietly in an encounter with this fear. I realize I've been trying to push it away, because my inner critic has been whispering that patients who are afraid, like patients who are depressed, don't do well. Now that I know he's been saying that, I can move. The rest of me knows I haven't been living steadily in a state of paralyzing fear, and that only if I receive and accept this fear will it shift of its own. There is no pressure, no deadline now, only my willingness to stay in the encounter. I am about to suggest that I make an image of the fear when I realize one is already present. It is very amorphous, washed-out pinkish stuff that fills the area in front of me. I'm surprised that the image itself isn't more threatening, but its taking up all my visual space is plenty threatening enough. I realize, too, that I have the child beside me and include her in my attention along with this pink nothingness. Now I mentally speak, although I don't have a clear idea of what other part of myself I may be addressing.

"It's very big and spread out, isn't it? Could it even be as big as panic?"

A small but clear voice answers, "Yeah. It could even be panic."

Suddenly there's a little letting go in my body. I'm not quite so engulfed. . . . Oh, my word. . . . There goes the image transforming spontaneously. In front of me now is a stunning sunset. A whole range of changing, brilliant pinks and reds. The washed-out pink expressed my feeling of overwhelming helplessness. The bright, varied colors have brought back life and movement. Released, I watch the sunset with pleasure and something like awe at the capacities of the human emotions and mind. The fear is much diminished and I know will resolve as the sun sets. I can get up and start my day.

*   *   *

My hair began to grow back after the third chemo. Among those who have seen it, perceptions vary: "Draft inductee," "Buddhist monk," and "Almost punk—a splash of magenta dye would clinch it." My own comment now that it is a half-inch long and actually able to go in different directions is, "Gracious, my hair is such a mess. I can't do a thing with it!" I am enchanted watching its progress, and with the warming weather look forward to the time when I can go without a hat. A while ago, I danced at a cast party. Theatre people predictably responded with enthusiasm to my lizard hat—but have you ever had to keep a hat on while dancing? Now that's hot!

*   *   *

I stand on a street corner as a clanging emergency vehicle roars by. I wait to see if more will follow. Beside me a woman shouts, "Oh, look," and I strain to search for a fire engine as she completes her sentence, "at the lizards on your hat!" My lizards have prompted many pleasurable social interchanges. Since the very popular lizard hat, the collection has enlarged to include a butterfly hat, a bird hat, and, zaniest of all, a hat with fish swimming around against a sea green cotton while a cat perched at top center surveys them, completely absorbed.

*   *   *

The day before going into my final chemo, I dream of a raggedy gray horse full of flailing pent-up energy coming at me and at other horses and a colt who are peacefully grazing. There's nothing mean or crazed about the horse, but I'm worried that it may run into me or the other horses, especially the colt. I leap on it bareback and find I am firmly seated. It is a wonderful feeling.

I share this dream with my hypnotherapist. We sometimes do other things than hypnosis, a rather eclectic approach. The friend who recommended her said she also did "expressive therapy." "What the deuce is that?" I asked, thinking that as a Californian, I'd pretty well heard of most things. I believe that galloping around the room, flailing my arms qualifies as expressive therapy! As I do this now in the session, I feel myself first as that pent-up horse, next as the firmly seated rider, and then I attend to the particular and unfamiliar quality of the flailing arms—hardly characteristic of either horse or rider. It is mostly a large outward movement; suddenly I get an unexpected association. Psychics, when they do a healing, make gathering and flicking-away gestures all around the body. This flailing feels like a grand version of that flicking away gesture. I flick off both the cancer and the toxicity of the chemo. I experience a grand moment of flicking off and finishing with all unhealthy stuff.

Refreshed and seated again, I'm curious about the gray color of the horse, a novel dream symbol combination for me. Gray is my color of gentle motherly nurturance (from a wonderful dream of a soft gray bird feeding its young). Yet here the gray is raggedy and associated with my horse of creative energy. My hypnotherapist laughs and says that, from where she sits, it sounds much the way my sprouting hair looks. Suddenly I have an experience of apparently unrelated things combining and integrating--my gray of nurturance, my horse of creative energy ready to be finished with chemo and cancer, right now pent-up and wanting to burst beyond my present state, and my growing hair, a sign of regeneration.

151

*   *   *

When I learn that my last chemo will be delayed because my white cell count is too low, I have a sudden flash: I could get away for a couple of days. Pacific Grove on the Monterey Peninsula, with its carpet of flowering electric pink ice plant by the ocean, fills my brain. Reality returns when I realize how low and uncertain my energy has been and the effort necessary for the trip. There must be a way to translate that image into something more manageable. I set up dates with friends to stroll in local gardens and parks. A former student, now a botanist, walks me through the gloriously blooming California native section of a local botanical garden. She is a delightful tour guide who points out many interesting details. "The iris family's wrap-around leaves are called 'equitant' from `equus,'" she tells me. "See how the leaves ride horsey-back on the main stem." My friends carry their mantle of learning lightly.

*   *   *

It's a strange paradox to be ecstatic when I find my white cell count is up and I can go into the hospital for my final chemo. After all, it is my least favorite indoor sport, coming even lower on the pleasure scale than cleaning out my sock drawer.

Once there, I find that even before anything is hitched up, I suddenly feel sick. I've never had the negative conditioning of chemo hit me so hard

152

before. I tell the nurse, and she assures me it won't be long before the anti-nausea medication is flowing into me. While I wait I begin to listen inside my body. It comes to me that though indeed I may be having some chemo conditioning sickness, I'm also having an anxiety attack. Instantly I know the cause. I have a roommate, a pleasant lady, but as I learn of her spreading cancer with lifelong alternating chemo and radiation, I'm hit by the horrid imagination of such a thing being my fate somewhere down the line.

I don't know why I tell the nurse, "I think more than feeling sick, I'm having an anxiety attack," but doing so makes me feel less engulfed by malaise. To my astonishment, she draws the privacy curtain, sits down on the bed and takes my hand. She just sits there with me for a spell of time, and though I feel I am trapped with the stimulus of my anxiety, something does ease. Something in the full awareness and acknowledgment, something in reporting the fact of my anxiety, though not the cause, something in the response of this caring other, helps.

My roommate has also shared that twice when she was on the last leg of extended chemo treatments, she totally broke down. "It's as if I'd held up all that time and suddenly I couldn't anymore. I even needed an emergency visit from the hospital psychotherapist." It makes sense to me. When the end is in sight, our systems tend to let down. And the more we've had to carry, the more there is built up that needs to be let out. Probably this is also happening to me now. I deeply appreciate and thank my roommate for sharing her experience with me. The human connection makes me feel less isolated.

Later I wonder if I would label an experience such as hers as "falling apart." Isn't it simply another, albeit thoroughly unpleasant, part of the flow of emotional events? We must have periodic release. It is legitimate to have an attack of distress at some points, and however intense, I am confident that *if received rather than fought off*, it will pass. Mine does pass.

Many of us have deeply ingrained training to be strong. In varying degrees, I think most of us have some discomfort with not being in control, with feeling weak, overwhelmed, or needy. These states feel like opposites and threats to being strong. But it is part of our humanness to feel sometimes weak, needy, or overwhelmed, and serious illness fundamentally threatens our sense of control. I believe it uses up our genuine strength and staying power if we try to deny or ward off such feelings, and that it is more frightening when we label ourselves as not being able to handle things. The late Virginia Satir once said, "We do not cope the same way when we are riding the bottom of the wave as when we are riding the top." I remind myself of her words when I find I am subtly giving myself the message that just because I'm in a rough place at the moment and not feeling "on top of things," I'm not coping. *I am still coping.* It is not the nature of the bottom of the wave to make us feel on top of things. Functioning under duress includes a whole range of resources and styles that may not be part of our ordinary repertoire. We need to welcome our ability to deal with the extraordinary in whatever unexpected ways we do. And we may gain some valuable new learning that expands our capacities and flexibility for ordinary living.

Now I remind myself that a series of waves, rough or gentle, will bring me to shore. Three days later I emerge, registering with quiet feeling that I did it: I am through chemotherapy! I know that when my body recuperates a little more and has a little more food in it, it will give me the full feeling of rejoicing.

Less than forty-eight hours later that feeling comes. Celebration most often includes calories or/and spending money. For me it always includes talk and sharing. Calories are not yet very interesting, but sharing with family and friends is. I give myself unbridled permission to make the long distance wires hum.

"This is Judy. I did it! I did it! I did it! I have finished my last chemotherapy! Whoopee!"

Love, Judy

Dear Reader,

Recently my oncologist asked if I'd talk with a patient who was going through a rough patch emotionally. It was my conversations with her that reminded me of an important issue. A diagnosis of cancer brings a jumble of fears, including fear of dying, loss of body parts or disfiguration, pain, upheaval in work, lifestyle, finances, and perhaps relationships. These are no small fears, but you may experience another fear that could be harder to define, and may be playing into other fears—namely the fear of losing yourself, your self-identity or self-esteem.

Some women know they have this fear. Others may not have identified it and may benefit from having it brought into the light. Perhaps there are patients for whom it plays little or no part, but I bet it's woven in, however subtly, for almost everyone.

Words are inadequate to define our sense of self, because it is made up of more than we can articulate. I see it as the core of each person. It's what makes each of us feel: *This is who I am; this is what makes me a worthwhile person; this is at the very center of the meaning of my life.* We can probably list some of the elements that make up our sense of self. It may include roles such as mother or partner, and self-images such as "sexy" or "in control," and it is even more informative if we define just what a role or self-image consists of personally. One person's "sexy" or "good mother" differs from another's and may be more or less affected by cancer. But unquestionably, cancer takes an especially hard toll on us if it threatens those things we identify as essential to who we are. So what aspects of this whole blooming business threaten *your* sense of self?

The most obvious cluster might be in the area of sexuality and feminine identity. Breast cancer treatment may affect sexual pleasure, appearance, and relationship with sex partners. All of us breast cancer patients have to grapple with these issues, but how deeply will vary. Depending on the nature of the cancer and treatment, they may be temporary discomforts or changes for life.

The negative impact of my first breast cancer on my sexuality and appearance was minor and short term. My breast was tender and hypersensitive if knocked against for some time, my lumpectomy scar was unnoticeable, my radiation suntan diminished with time, and I looked normal when dressed. I even enjoyed heightened pleasure in the nipple for about a year after radiation. However, my second cancer changed my life forever. The double mastectomy felt like a significant loss to my sexuality. On the plus side were my long, committed relationship with my husband and the fact that I was clear about sacrificing my breasts to save my life.

As a person who lives a high-on-comfort, low-on-fashion life, I never investigated wearing prostheses. I experienced a spell of mild self-consciousness about my flat chest, but now it is as totally me as were large breasts previously. If I had lost the benefit of breasts, then I was going to revel in the freedom from the discomfort of harnessing bras—certainly not replace them with another nuisance! After the amount of medical intrusion into my body, I had no desire to do reconstruction surgery. Though I never said it in so many words, there's no way of knowing what life span is ahead of me, and I wanted to get back to physical well-being as soon as possible and enjoy it for as long as possible. My choices were made before questions arose about the safety of breast implants, so that was not a consideration. Although I miss the appearance, and, more importantly, the pleasure of breasts, and occasionally still feel the sting of my losses, my sense of self was not impaired. This is an example of what might potentially be the greatest threat to self-identity turning out not to be so. For another woman, it might cause a greater threat to self-identity. How your sexual partner feels about and deals with it and how openly you can talk about it will also be factors. But loss is loss. If we encounter whatever the losses are, I think ultimately we'll find the self intact. (I see *encounter* as a series of small, not necessarily, recognizable steps. Your reading and musing about this may be part of your encounter).

Threat to self, especially to sexual self-image, might even be a determining factor in choice of treatment. This is particularly true if mastectomy is recommended. The woman my oncologist put in touch with me told me she had said to him, "If you save my life, but lose me, the person, you haven't done me any favors." She was relieved that her concern was received as an important factor in how they should proceed—and I give a big thumbs-up to my doctor for his responsiveness to her as a whole person.

The issue of fear of loss of self may not be fully understood or valued by family, friends, and even some doctors. They all want you to get well, and their anxiety is often best alleviated by knowing that you're "doing all the right things" and "have a wonderful attitude." They may not be aware that this could put pressure on you. Some of your divergences from these models of perfection may be connected to fear of loss of self. The more you can identify which things threaten your sense of self, the more you will be able to make your choices consciously, explain your needs to others, and when necessary, protect yourself from well-meaning people who pressure you.

What about loss of hair? It can not only alter our sense of femininity, but so changes our face that it can make us feel not like ourselves. Wearing a wig made me feel framed by something alien and artificial as well as physically uncomfortable. In contrast, my colorful, goofy hats suited my sense of self and allowed its playful aspect to shine. Wigs may be less of a problem for women who wear them purely for style or for whom time spent on hairdos and makeup is an integral part of their day. I found I would have been more threatened if my hair hadn't grown back than I was by the loss of breasts. I never would have guessed that in advance. Perhaps we are more adaptable than we realize; I was called on to say only a temporary good-bye to my hair, but I had to deal with the permanent loss of my breasts.

Does the intrusion of cancer on your work, your professional life, and your creative life also affect your sense of self? For me, the diagnosis of cancer interrupting the book I was writing was a major threat to my sense of self. Although that book got stashed, and I didn't encounter my grief about it until two years later when looking to see if parts of it could be incorporated into this book, writing the cancer letters kept my identity as a writer.

Which other aspects of your situation threaten your sense of self? Losing accustomed independence and self-sufficiency? Being forever peered at and poked in a partially undressed state? Let's face it: Heads of state and corporate powerhouses do not do business in hospital gowns. Even if you do not feel the need to dress for success, the hospital gown does not clothe your self-image!

Your sense of self could also be threatened by distressed or angry feelings popping out when and where you'd rather they didn't. You may attach a lot to feeling in control. Cancer sure gets in the way of that! What about the phrases "having cancer," "being sick," and "being a cancer patient"? You may identify yourself as a healthy person who doesn't fuss and complain, and suddenly you may feel like a fusser and complainer.

You may think of things that are particular to you that you can't imagine anyone else understanding, not even another person with breast cancer. Be sure to name and honor those things too. When you've covered the easily named things that feel important to your sense of self, you might ask if that covers it or if there is something you haven't yet gotten hold of. You might open up to further discovery by spending time with some sense you have of yourself that you may not yet have words to describe. Slop around on the paper with messy prose or scribbled drawings or ask a good, non-interfering listener to let you explore the question aloud. Try taking a moment to listen inside your body and see if anything comes into awareness, and then see if you can describe what it is, or just be with the feeling. I recall touching a deep sense of myself when doing impromptu expressive movement in my living room. What came was something like: I'm here inside myself, right at my own center, whole and free, in the midst of all this cancer treatment whirligig.

*   *   *

Although I see the self as ongoing through our lives, different facets may be important at different times. We may feel more grounded in the self and more "like ourselves" in some stages of life than in others. You may also want to include an assessment of how grounded or off balance your sense of self feels.

How hard cancer, or any crisis, hits emotionally is greatly affected by where we are in life when it strikes, and where we are in relation to self and our deepest personal meanings. What stage of life are/were you in at the time of diagnosis and treatment, and what defines you in this period?

Are you in middle age, perhaps dealing with aging parents, teenagers' problems, or other major demands? Are you experiencing the empty nest or/and midlife crisis, trying to figure out where to go from here, perhaps feeling that you've lost a familiar sense of self and not yet forged a new one? Are you in a bumpy place in your primary relationship or in your work? Are you in full rush in a career that needs you to give your all? Are you just starting a new relationship? Have you left an old relationship without a new one yet on the horizon, but are hoping for one? Have you daughters whose cancer risk is higher now, or who are developing breasts just as you are having breast disease? Are you among the now-younger generation of women getting breast cancer in their thirties and early forties, occasionally even in their twenties? Are treatments bringing on an early menopause? Are you pregnant? Have you a new baby or young children? Have you just gotten a lot of stuff behind you and were ready to embark or just embarked on something new? Are you grappling with problems of aging? Does cancer come on top of other health problems? Are you grieving for the death of a spouse or someone else important? Have you just moved to a new house, living arrangement, or community? Or is this a time that is fairly stable? There's no such thing as a good time to get cancer, but timing and some conditions in your life can certainly add to or ease the burden.

As you contemplate the phase of your life in which cancer struck, allow yourself to step back and see what your timing and circumstances look like. What are the particular meanings for you? Do they threaten your self-identity? Acknowledge whatever is nasty in your situation. "No wonder I'm having a rough time," you might say. "As if it's not bad enough to have cancer, it's coming at this time when. . . ."

As you look at those things which make the particular moment difficult, you might also see if there are aspects of your life and sense of self that offer support. For instance, I had gone through menopause about a year before my diagnosis, so I not only didn't have to deal with the physiological and emotional effects of chemo-induced menopause, but also had largely ridden out the bumpiest issues of aging and self connected to that passage.

You may also want to consider what aspects of your self are alive and well in spite of crisis. Are there things you thought would threaten you deeply and turned out not to? Are you finding some new strength and shift of meaning as you take on this challenge?

During my first cancer I worked on my timidity about telephoning doctors to ask something I forgot when I was there. I realized the distance I had traveled on this issue when, a few months ago, a pain in my arm suddenly triggered cancer fears. My rational self thought it highly unlikely and that my anxiety was piggybacking on other anxieties. Even though I had a regular checkup in ten days, I telephoned to talk to someone rather than live with unnecessary fear.

Give yourself credit when you see such a change in your behavior.

And remember that whenever you make a conscious choice of small daring, it yields the benefit of personal growth that outlasts the crisis. The very things that threaten your sense of self may well be the cause not of loss of self, but rather of deepening of self.

Although your view of yourself may get shaken up, you may also discover that your self-identity goes deeper than the things you thought it depended on. I believe that whatever you face and whatever you bring to your encounter will enrich and strengthen the very self you may fear to lose.

Here's to your self: the one you have already developed, are enriching, and will come to know better because of your experience.

Love, Judy

July 9

Dear Friends,

This is a time of transition. I feel joyful to be let off the hook—quite literally—of chemo and mildly resistant to having to do anything more. It's also a time of some background anxiety as I will have a test, or maybe more than one, to see if there are any indications of cancer.

* * *

I have the long-anticipated, celebrative visit of my college roommate and her husband, en route home to the east coast from China. While they are here, our '63 VW bug is stolen. The theft complicates John's life extraordinarily, and for both of us it is an emotional loss. It was my first and only car until 1982. It took us on our honeymoon. In recent years, it has taken John—and sometimes his canoe on top, hanging fore and aft— all over California and to Canada. It is a nasty event to fall into this time of celebration. We feel violated, hurt, and angry. I listen inside: Do I also feel a loss of a piece of myself? No. After the events of the last eight months, I discover my sense of self is so clearly centered within me that much as I feel hurt and sorrow, no part of me has been stolen with the car.

* * *

A friend invites me to a dress rehearsal of a flamenco dance performance she is in. Sitting on a folding chair in a ramshackle dance studio, I catch the vitality of women whose entire attention is focused on creative physical expression. I marvel at a world not dominated by full-time health care. Though not professionals, these skilled, long-practiced artists have both flare and control. They dance with all the fire of femininity that is flamenco.

Whenever I watch dancing, I fantasize myself doing it. On this occasion, the fantasy collides with new realities. I have no breasts and no hair to speak of; I'm flabby, dumpy, and out of condition. As a physical specimen of femininity, I'm a pretty funny-looking bird. Momentarily I alight on the question, "Will I have breasts again?" I'm far from ready to even consider if I will do reconstruction surgery. The question dissipates as the arched backs, the swirling colors of long skirts, fringed shawls, and oversized earrings pull me back into the dance. The intense rhythms of guitar, clapping hands, "Cante Hondo" singing, and clacking feet take me into deep, thrumming awareness. I am that sound, that color, that flashing grace. I am that feminine fire. Dance, ladies, dance. I love you and I am you.

* * *

I dream of strong winds blowing up. Perhaps a hurricane is coming. I'm near the ocean with its heavy wave action and anxious about where I'll be when the full blast hits. Then I'm standing under a huge concrete building in an area like an underground parking lot. People are cutting through the thick, square concrete pillars that support the building. Tipping at an angle, the whole building is coming down intact as a unit. Already one corner, where the stanchions have been cut, touches the ground. I'm a little angry that they're doing this, especially with high winds increasing.

When I first wake, I worry that these symbols might mean that tests will reveal more cancer, because my anxiety about test results is near the surface. Even I, who have extensive experience in dream interpretation, can get caught by the conscious mind jumping to its habitual perceptions. But as I stay with the dream, I recall that winds in my dreams have always been the winds of positive change. Now, as I feel the excitement of those winds, I note that I am unscathed by the toppling building, which is coming down easily in one piece. Suddenly I know that this great structure is being brought down intentionally by decisive parts of my unconscious. It is the big letting-down of the superstructure of cancer treatment I have had to hold up for the past eight months. My whole body feels the release and joy. I thank my unconscious for its beautiful piece of work.

*   *   *

I hit the nadir and seem to drag a long time. It may also be the effect of the deeper let down at the end of chemotherapy. I have to write reassuringly in my journal because my critic doesn't like my being tired a lot. I also eat more to combat the fatigue and he doesn't like the resulting weight gain either! I remind myself that I need to modify my expectations and focus on enjoyment in little moments and little activities. I remind myself *not to try to get ahead of where I am.*

*　　*　　*

I dream of an evergreen to be used as a Christmas tree. It looks quite ratty and I'm trying to identify it. The needles look like hemlock, but the cones have the distinctive bracts of the Douglas fir. A woman tells me with great certainty its name, which I've never heard before, something like Santa Teresa. Remarkable for any tree is a white magnolia-like flower blossoming out of one of the cones. As I try to make sense of the tree's mixed information, I notice that only the bottom part looks old and ratty. The top is a healthy fresh green and is growing vigorously. It's not such a poor specimen after all! Hmm. And it is out of the tired lower part that the flowering cone is growing—that seed carrier of new life already blossoming.

I believe this dream is pointing to my being healthy and cancer-free. In the past, my dream trees have had an archetypal quality of life. This tree also reflects my present ratty-edged fatigue, which I have certainly come by honestly and which will pass whenever it is ready. For now, it needs to be received and honored, not pushed and judged. I again pause to accept fully my present state and feel the easing that acceptance brings. I muse further that the needles look rather like those of the real-life Santa Lucia fir, which is close to the dream name of the tree. The Santa Lucia is a splendid, lofty tree that seems to have the quality of wisdom of the ages and spirit within. Finally I note the presence of the woman who identifies the tree. The dream suggests that a part of me knows something of a different order than the conscious Judy knows.

*　　*　　*

In my doctor's waiting room I run into the hospital roommate I mentioned in the last letter. She asks if what happened to me in the hospital was an anxiety attack. I say yes and let her know how helpful she was. But I feel awkward in the full, silent waiting room, and perhaps for fear of saying the wrong thing, I do not divulge that the cause of my attack was her ill health. Afterward I feel dissatisfied and wish I had been able to say more.

Another day, I'm given a second chance. This time I waylay my former roommate in the more private corridor. I tell her how much I admire her courageous handling of being in perpetual treatment, and that my anxiety attack was due to imagining myself having to go through something similar. Our conversation is a gift to us both. Whenever we can express what we feel simply and with compassion and respect, it breaks down isolation.

*　　*　　*

I dream that a garment I sent for has arrived in the mail. I expected a jacket but to my astonishment, it is a full-length coat. I try it on and its long, clean lines are very becoming. Only awake do I register the most wonderful feature: It is green, my color of healing. I rejoice in its color and the fact that it is a full-length, body-covering garment. I welcome this beautiful green coat.

*　　*　　*

I go for a preliminary appointment with my radiation oncologist. We're old buddies, but I haven't seen him for a year since our semi-annual appointment was overridden by the cancer discovered in the fall. He has, of course, been receiving these letters, and wrote me one of encouragement after receiving the first one. I am grateful that he is in a different hospital. People and medical care have been wonderful at my other hospital, but as my body has had an overdose of unpleasant experiences there, it is good to go now to an "uncontaminated" environment. From the radiation I did here four and a half years ago, I have positive associations with people and no negative conditioning to my body. I am completely caught off guard, therefore, when I innocently put on the gown left for me. Woof! There's that same unpleasant, now chemo-linked, nauseating smell as in my other hospital gowns and bedclothes. I pull off the gown, toss it

172

in the soiled linen bin, and put my shirt back on. No way will I wear a gown for daily radiation if I don't want to end up with more negative conditioning. The doctor is characteristically genial and accommodating on the subject.

I model several of my hats. Taking in lizards, birds, butterflies, cats, and fish with full appreciation, he allows as how maybe it would be best to schedule me after regular hours to avoid alarming other patients! He doesn't need to give me as much detailed information as before the first radiation, but he does have to toss in the standard bit that there is no guarantee of success. Then he adds and stresses a point which I consider to be another example of the good doctoring I have.

"Because radiation is done in order to save the breast, we don't usually have the certain information that pathology reports afford. But because of your double mastectomy and the subsequent pathology report showing that the left breast was free of cancer, we know we have a history of radiation success with you." His words help me to go into treatment with minimal anxieties and maximum positive expectations.

*   *   *

The day after I see the radiation oncologist, I wake with a sore throat and swollen glands, and by evening it is evident that I am coming down with something. By the calendar I should be beyond the nadir, but I only recently started to feel perkier, and now this. Damn. At dinner I feel low

173

and find it hard to imagine anything that could make me feel cheerful again until I feel physically well. The phone rings. John answers, turns toward me, and gives a vigorous thumbs-up sign. I can tell by that and his end of the conversation that the VW bug has been found! Wowie! It is almost two weeks since it was stolen and we were not holding our breath. We are both beaming, especially as the car is in good condition. I was wrong that it would take physical well-being to cheer me up.

*   *   *

My flu takes my voice away completely for a couple of days, yet even this low energy is more comfortable than the dragginess of the nadir. We have a glorious after-the-season rain, perhaps the best of this whole drought year. I need variety in weather and miss rain even during California's normal six dry months. Since the drought, I feel truly deprived. Now the gray world wraps itself around me like a comforting blanket. The hypnotic sound of the rain draws me deep into relaxation and contentment. Seated in front of a bookcase, I pull out not only books to get rid of, but notebooks from past eras. As I leaf through dusty pages, I drop into French and Spanish classes from college, Mexico, France, and Switzerland. With other notebooks I re-enter my fifteen years of teaching. I proceed to my forties as I look through notebooks from classes in hypnosis and writing. I am transported on a gentle voyage to many places of my past and find it unaccustomedly easy to let go of the paraphernalia of it. I am suiting my level of activity perfectly to my physical needs and am refreshed by the trancelike state induced by rain and memories.

*   *   *

Though the post-chemo blood counts are fine for radiation, I delay it an extra week in order to recover fully from the flu and to get away a couple of times before being held down to the daily treatments. Through this time I am waiting for the results of the CA 15-3 tumor-indicator blood test. Hope and anxiety flutter in the background of whatever I am doing.

John drives me to the vineyard of a friend with whom he makes wine in the Napa Valley. It is an easy outing with no preparation and minimal physical effort for me. It is a beautiful day, comfortably warm, but not yet hot as Napa can be in summer. We spend a major part of our time sitting on a deck looking into oak trees draped with Spanish moss. An intermittent wind sends clouds scudding across the sky, giving us dappled light. A gentle walk takes us among late-blooming wildflowers. We ride home in the early evening while it is still light. Magically, we head into an almost full moon that dominates the sky in front of us. Suddenly I am struck by the generosity of this landscape with its tended fresh green vineyards, tree-covered hills, and winding creek. I feel tears, and say to John how much that word *generosity* means. "I have experienced enormous generosity from people throughout these last eight months, but my physical environment has been limited and ungiving." The contrast of hospital rooms, doctors' waiting rooms, and operating rooms with this singing piece of nature moves me. It has been a day in another world, a day out of time.

*   *   *

I dream I'm standing on an edge of land that drops off sheerly to the ocean. Apparently something came along that wiped out whatever structures separated land from sea and provided protection from falling over. Out of cracks in the asphalt of this razed area, I see a luminous flowering shrub growing—an exciting image of life regenerating. I've seen its real counterpart occasionally on driving trips to the Sierra foothills and on our recent day in Napa, but never where I could stop and get out of the car. As we drove by, the brilliant yellow flowers looked as though they might be of the pea family, and a splash of maroon something added flare. I'm lured by the image of this beautiful shrub growing out of the place where the structures separating land and sea (conscious and unconscious? life and death? known and unknown? safety and danger?) were knocked away by cancer.

Awake and driving in a town over the hills a few days later, I spot a specimen of my mysterious shrub on a front lawn. Quickened by the meeting of dreaming and waking realities, and because someone is in the yard, I pull over and get out. It is an exuberant, magical shrub up close, this one a small tree with slender branches and unmistakable pea family flowers and leaves. The splash of maroon is the flaming plumes of stamens shooting out from the center of the intense yellow flowers. The owner says it is called Bird of Paradise. Well, he is a stranger. I don't throw my arms around him and tell him just how much that name thrills me or bend his ear about my dream, but I do sail off, exhilarated to have met my pizzazzy shrub of new life.

*　　*　　*

John and I go to the oncologist. The first order of business is to hear the results of the CA 15-3 tumor-indicator blood test. It is normal! Oh, Wow! Oh, Wonder! Oh, Expanding Universe! I go over and plunk a kiss on my doctor's cheek and do a little soft-shoe so the sheer bursting emotion won't interfere with my mental processes. Then I muster my brain power to ask how this test works. It measures antibody activity, and I have already been warned by a post-treatment friend who has it frequently that it can go above the normal range one time, causing anxiety, then return to normal. My doctor explains that although it is not perfect, it tends to show false positives more often than false negatives, and that using it monitors for ongoing significant change that could indicate the presence of cancer. Having this test monthly is part of my future of living with the shadow of cancer, but right now *I don't have cancer! I don't have cancer!* The chemotherapy has done its work! My labors have been worthwhile!

Before radiation begins I have one more treat, an overnight visit with friends over the hills to go to the annual Rodeo Day parade the next morning. We've done this for a number of years, so it's another familiar piece of my life retrieved. Speaking of their daughter who is gloriously in love, I say expansively, "There's nothing more wonderful than being in love, nothing . . . *except not having cancer!*"

Love, Judy

Dear Reader,

Dreams have long been a wonderful source of support and delight for me and perhaps they are or can become so for you. They offer a symbol-rich and often sensory-rich balance to the rush and go of ordinary life and the drabness of treatment, hospital, and waiting rooms. They remind me how much the unconscious is doing on my behalf, and are often ahead of my waking knowledge. If I keep in touch with my dreams, they offer me guidance, solace, and encouragement.

Interpreting dreams can take time, especially initially. Keep in mind that you may sometimes feel muddled and full of the feelings of the dream as you work to decipher its meaning. In my letters, my dreams are tidily narrated after their meaning was clear to me. I assure you that while deciphering, I often feel muddled, sometimes even agitated, but I trust the process and love its rewards. With experience, the language of the unconscious may come to feel as familiar as a foreign language in which you first felt awkward and have now become fluent—though you may always enjoy a sense of wonder at the creativity of that language, and you will not always understand it!

My own process owes a lot to the work of both Carl Jung and Eugene Gendlin. What I say here can be only an hors d'oeuvre—a teaser to lure you to dreamwork if you are a novice or a new idea or two if you're experienced. I want first to introduce some attitudes and approaches that may help you deal with the frightening and difficult aspects of dreams, then tell you some of the ways that I go about working on them.

*   *   *

Dreams communicate by symbols. They usually offer us something we don't already know or something to support and strengthen positive growth. The greatest stumbling blocks to dream interpretation are the tendencies of the waking mind to be too literal and to jump to its habitual perceptions. So if your mind offers an old familiar interpretation, or one that is literal, negative, or self-critical, you have probably not gotten what the dream is offering. Set it aside and continue to ask questions or look at another part of the dream that may reveal something fresh.

How do you know whether you've got an interpretation right, especially if you're a beginner? You don't always. Sometimes you may just hold two possibilities, even opposite ones, and go on to another part of the dream or some further questions and see what evolves. But here's something that might help. When you've got a right meaning, you may experience a shift inside your body. It may be barely noticeable or a real little letting go.

You get such a feeling in your body when you've been trying to recall something you were meant to do or take with you. You review possibilities in your mind, and when you hit upon the right answer, you feel a That's-it! response in your body. When you hit on the right meaning of a dream or any aspect of it, you may also get such a physical shift. If your interpretations are coming only from your head, try paying attention inside your body and see if your interpretation gives you that little "yes" feeling of release.

Dreams are by no means always pleasant, and yet even unpleasant ones may offer the dreamer something positive. Sometimes dream symbols take frightening forms like fires, avalanches, floods, or killings because their language is metaphoric and dramatic, like that of myths and fairy tales. They may also be frightening because we are afraid of an unknown or unaccepted part of us they are presenting.

For instance, a dream figure who is nastily aggressive may contain the germ of healthy assertiveness the dreamer needs to cultivate. If you were taught that stating your needs or ideas wasn't nice, your dream may cloak assertiveness in a negative figure or an excessive behavior. If you recoil at such a dream, try asking if just some of that quality, probably in a different form, could be a positive thing.

A technique that can help break the habitual perceptions of your conscious mind, particularly if you're not learning anything new or if the dream is frightening or distasteful, is to try an opposite interpretation. My dream of high winds in the previous letter felt threatening, yet they were winds of positive change. Had I not recalled that symbol from the past, I could have asked, "Might this thing that feels threatening be something good happening?"

The following bad dream I had years ago illustrates several of these points.

I dreamed of being terrorized by a man trying to get into my house and woke with my heart pounding. Writing in my journal, I asked him who he was and what he wanted. To my surprise, he answered that *he* was afraid, shut outside alone, and wanted to come in and be protected in my house. That showed me that a figure whom I found frightening was a rejected part of myself that needed my acceptance, understanding, and kindness in order to grow into something healthy, able, and balanced. Often frightening figures that hound us in dreams are parts of us that we have cut off, and they resort to extreme measures to get our attention.

*   *   *

Because writing taps more than my immediate consciousness, I not only write down my dreams, but continue to write as a way to discover their meaning. If you do this, you will find yourself remembering more and having more meanings open up spontaneously. It will also encourage the dreaming process. Even a wisp is worth recording, for sometimes more will come to mind as you write. Telling your dream to a friend is often helpful, so long as it is someone who won't take over the interpreting. Talking into a tape recorder might also work.

You can get down all that you remember as a first step; or if words and phrases begin to reveal more significance or set associations in motion, you can let go of recording the whole and explore whatever feature is yielding something new. Describe and muse on whatever lures you: a character, a color or the way colors are combined with each other or other features, an animal, an object, an image, an action, a place, or the relationship between any of those elements. Anything sharp or vague that draws your attention, especially by a detail that is unlikely to the conscious mind or outright contrary to reality is food for thought. Listen for any associations that arise spontaneously as you go along; or at the end of your writing, ask yourself what in your life is like this.

If it's an unknown person or thing, describe it until you get a sense of what quality is important. If it's a known person, make associations, or describe until you feel which aspect of the person is the pertinent symbol in this dream. Don't worry if you don't get interpretations for everything. Even after you have quite a lot of experience, some things don't yield. I think noting them helps you gain skill in the process, and sometimes you can go back later and see more of what a dream is about. Over a period of days or weeks, you may see a trend and the subject will become clear.

You can ask a dream figure, animal, or thing questions and let it answer in writing, as I did with the frightening man breaking into my house. I often don't expect this to work, fearing that my conscious mind will answer. I am almost always gratified to find that the answers bring something new.

Place, atmosphere, mood, and weather can all be evocative. Poke around to find the right adjectives or phrases to describe the setting or mood. You can even invite words and phrases to come when you wake with a vague or strong feeling but can't recall the content of the dream. Sometimes, content will then spring to mind. If it doesn't, try asking, "Is there something in my life that feels like that?"

My most fundamental assumption is that the people, things, and animals in my dreams are parts of me. Once in a while, if a dream figure is a real person who is very close to me and with whom I have a complex, long-term relationship, I include the possibility that the dream may or may *also* be about that relationship. But even if I dream about my husband, I still ask questions to find out if this dream John is "some John part of me." All my friends and my sisters and cousins appear as dream parts of me. My parents, now long dead, are also most often deeply integrated parts of me. See if this way of looking at dream figures helps you.

Animals often represent instinctual, primitive, or emotional parts. Even before being introduced to the dog as a Jungian symbol of instinct, I had pegged my dream dogs as an expression of very basic needs and natural ways of functioning. After the diagnosis of my first cancer, I dreamed an alligator had gotten into my house and that I was trying to get it out. I was much too threatened to do anything other than create further imagery to "get it gone!" Although this is one good way of responding to an image of cancer, at this distance I would like to imagine asking the alligator where it came from, and why, and what it needed in order to transform and heal. Sometimes an image will transform spontaneously when we work with it.

Children, babies, young animals, or new plants may express something just coming into being. A child might also be a child part of you. Old and dying people may be things that are dying in you because you are ready to let them go to make way for the new.

If you do a lot of dreamwork, you may find images recurring. This can help you discover the meaning of a symbol over time, and once understood that symbol may reappear like a known shorthand mark. Cats, dogs, and horses are all shorthand for me now as are most colors. It is a good idea, though, to hold such shorthand lightly, and see if it does unlock the meaning of the particular dream. This is especially true of people. As they change or your relationship to them opens up, their symbolism may alter accordingly. When one person, who had represented a fearful and self-limiting part of me, grew and took a leap toward a fuller life, I noticed that she also changed as a dream figure to represent an evolving part of me.

After you have gleaned meaning from the dream, you may find it useful to continue from where the dream left off or to go in a different direction with it. Once I discovered that the man I shut out in my dream needed to be welcomed, I imagined letting him in and befriending him. This kind of invitation can be particularly powerful if done in writing, or in your head, before sleep. The dream has given you information. Now you can consciously help develop what you have learned. You can even do it when you feel the positive power of a symbol but haven't yet understood exactly what it refers to in your life.

If all of this sounds like a lot of work, keep in mind that it can also be play. Don't feel you have to decipher a whole dream. Sometimes you get a lovely piece of meaning out of just a wisp of an image. And whenever you get new meaning, revel in it. Call it back to mind, along with its feeling, off and on through the day. Doing so helps strengthen in you the new thing the dream is presenting. During treatment I carried all my healing and supportive dreams with me through the day and sometimes for several days.

Appreciating and thanking the dream for whatever it has brought encourages the dreaming process. It also helps to undercut a feeling that your work is incomplete just because you didn't decipher the entire dream. I have come to feel that dreams are like waves—individual, ever-renewing parts of something larger—and the ongoing process will bring more from that ocean of the unconscious.

Sweet dreams. And remember, even the "bad" ones, once understood, may be magical and healing.

Love, Judy

October 18

Dear Friends,

    This letter has taken longer to complete because the quality and pace of my life have changed since treatment ended. I've also been trying to foresee if this is to be the last letter. If so, perhaps I've been putting off the act of bringing closure. I dislike ending relationships, and unmistakably these letters have woven relationship and community for me. They have also given me a singular experience of writing, which is usually a lone occupation with relatively little and much-delayed response. In addition to the tremendous healing support and caring you have given to Judy, the cancer patient, you have unwittingly given tremendous response to Judy, the writer. For all this I expect to go through some withdrawal pains, but now it is time to continue the story to date.

*   *   *

    Before starting radiation, I buy a set of red towels and collect a variety of red shirts to wear because the dark red dye the technologists will use to mark my body sometimes stains fabric. About the same time the weather warms up, so I stop wearing my hats and let the world view my peculiarly brief but growing hair.

    Radiation takes place at 11:00 a.m., five days a week, from June 11 to July 18. It is a daily spirited tea party. I expected as much because even though some of the crew is new, I know the vibes in this place. I know these will be people who can relate. Daily I exchange pleasant words with the parking attendant who directs me to a space. I choose to climb the several flights of stairs rather than use the elevator, pleased with my growing physical stamina. I sail into the radiation room, pull off my shirt, and lie down on the table. We exchange humor and goodwill as the members of the crew execute the intricate steps of their technological dance. The machine makes its characteristic whining whirr, while I stare at the stars and comets imaginatively placed by one of the techs on the ceiling.

What's new this time is that every other day I have a square of gold lamé laid across the part of my chest that is treated. One of the techs refers to this as "fancy day." I get a lot of mileage out of the fantasy of being dressed up in the ultimate forties'-style evening gown.

Partway through treatment the protocol will change and there won't be any more "fancy days." To celebrate my last gold lamé experience, I dig out the gold tinsel wig I got at a county fair last year. It is a marvelous, outrageous coif with gold bangs that come well down the forehead and locks that flutter at mid-neck. To wear it is to bring out my utmost foolishness. The doctor, appreciative as always, says in mock resignation, "I *try* to run a respectable establishment here." And indeed, the wig could certainly suggest the more lurid aspects of a seamy nightlife. As we chat our way through the radiation set-up procedures, I say to the two crew members, "Well you know, they always say blondes have more fun."

I'm having such a good time with the wig that I also wear it to my oncologist's. Now this takes more inner centering and keeping my eye clearly on my goal, because an oncologist's waiting room is not a barrel of laughs. Furthermore, I look like a bag lady as I have a ratty shopping bag overflowing with goodies I am taking to the office staff that day as my token of appreciation for all they do. When my oncologist, whom I haven't seen since before the beginning of radiation, comes to the door to call me in, I greet him warmly and say, "I just thought you'd like to see how my hair has grown out since I last saw you."

*　　*　　*

I continue to feel fine with no side effects of any sort, nothing reminiscent of my other radiation experience. I level with my radiation doctor: "I've put a detective on your trail, because I don't think you're doing radiation."

"Well," he answers, calmly equal to the accusation, "we've learned that patients don't like side effects, so we just go through the motions." I then start to ask questions, wanting to know why this is unlike the last time. Of course treating a flat surface rather than a large amount of breast tissue makes a significant difference, but I'd like to think there may be other reasons. Suddenly in mid-query, I realize this is no time to risk hearing any information that could give my unconscious even the slightest negative suggestion to pick up on. We will go for reinforcing the current positive experience and leave intellectual curiosity alone.

What's in the back of my mind is wondering whether my new habit of daily meditation may be contributing to my doing so well. In the second week of radiation, I took myself to a local meditation center to learn the skill. I go to my radiation appointment right after my morning routine, so now my daily list starts:

1) Walk
2) Meditate
3) Radiate

I feel that meditation along with now-regular exercise is giving me more balance, energy, and calm alertness.

*   *   *

While I'm in radiation, an idea begins to sizzle—something new I'd like to add to my life. After some recovery time, I want to start a group for cancer patients who'd like to use writing as a means of self-support and processing their experience. I get excited as I explore the things I'd like to offer and the skills at my disposal to create such a class: my fifteen years as a teacher (which I have missed since writing), my writer self, my broad and deep travels in the land of the psyche, and my coming through two cancers.

The end of radiation in sight with only a pinkening of the skin which is not painful or hot, I need to consider how to mark my final day. At the end of last time's radiation, I rented a mortar board and made a one person procession, intoning "Pomp and Circumstance" down the inner corridor from waiting room to radiation room. Suddenly it strikes me what is absolutely organic to this ending.

Carrying my bag lady shopping bag to my final appointment, I whisk myself unnoticed into the bathroom. First I pin a flurry of ribbons on the front of my shirt, so they dangle and flutter celebratively. Then I start the careful process of putting on the nine hats that were made for me and have carried me through the many months of treatment. I have to build slowly, pulling each down as securely as possible, putting the most fragile butterfly hat on last, then topping it gently with the gold tinsel wig. Carefully I walk out into the corridor and greet the crew waiting in the control room. Such is their response that the rest of the techs, who are between patients, emerge from the other control room to see what is going on, until all have converged into the corridor. It is the perfect moment to present them with the thank you goodies from my bag and for them to take pictures. They, in turn, present me with a photocopied diploma.

College of Radiation Oncology

The Fellows and Ladies of this College (a.k.a. "Hardknocks")
on recommendation of the Radiation Therapy Technologists,
and by Virtue of the Authority in them Vested, Confer upon

Judith Hart

who has endured all manner of pain, frustration, wily witti-
cisms of the technologists, weary waiting room "weather" talk,
ancient and venerable reading material in the aforementioned
room, and the stares and inane remarks of the population at
large; and has satisfactorily pursued the prescribed course, and
prescribed prescriptions, and has now passed the required
examinations and X-rays for the degree of

"One Tough Cookie"

with all the rights, privileges, honors and side-effects apper-
taining to this degree.

(Dated and signed by technologist and doctor)

The doctor also is suitably rewarding in his response, looking "nervously" up and down the empty corridor like a spy hoping to make safe passage, then sticking his head into the front office and saying to the secretary, "Would you please see to it that nobody comes in the department until Mrs. Hart leaves."

At the end of the appointment, my hats and ribbons piled back into the shopping bag, and clutching my diploma, I walk out of ten months of cancer treatment.

*   *   *

Three days after radiation John and I go to a wedding. Under the best of circumstances I have difficulty dressing up, but I do own one knock-'em-dead outfit. Suspecting I might run into problems, I tried it on the week before. My weight gain made it impossible to get into the linen pants.

The raw silk top with its darts carefully fitted to my former person hung too strangely to wear. This left only the smashing red linen jacket and red hat which, because of sketchy hair, tended to slide down over my eyes. I rustled around my closet to find another top and pants that, though hardly as effective, would do. But when the day comes, I am assaulted by uncomfortable feelings. This is my first dress-up public occasion since losing my breasts. Suddenly my flat chest, skimpy hair, overweight body, and inability to wear my whole outfit make me feel like a picked chicken about to be set down among prize plumed birds at the county fair. I rummage around and add pizzazz with chest-covering gold necklaces bought at a Greek dance festival. I find a way to angle the hat so I can see out. Now the outfit begins to look more like me. By the time the dance band strikes up, I am in full form and dance every dance.

*   *   *

One of the issues cancer patients ending successful treatment face is concern for future health, particularly if their disease, like mine, shows a high statistical rate of recurrence. It's natural to want to do everything possible to prevent recurrence. It's sometimes difficult to distinguish between what may be useful and what is merely haring off after snake oil. I don't have the temperament of a "true believer" in any one thing, but I do believe that enriching my emotional and spiritual process can contribute to the health of my body. I have been pleased with meditation. Now I want to learn an advanced health-oriented technique that is taught to meditators.

I call to find out when and where the next West Coast class will be and learn that one is scheduled for Reno about a week after I finish radiation. A healing pilgrimage to Reno! What a hilarious, spiffy, charming idea! The timing feels right for my first little driving trip in over a year.

I stop overnight at a friend's on the way. The next day's drive is tiring and I go to bed at 6:30. The following day I enjoy dropping into a cool, sheltered, meditational world, and I get what I've come for. I emerge into the glaring desert sun which, a few hours later, gives way to the jazzy neon colors of Reno at night.

I revel in my fresh and tender freedom and the sheer excitement of ordinary experience. Just eating in an unremarkable restaurant makes me feel as happy and proud as a small child admitted into the glamorous adult world. I drink in the aliveness of summer tourists: at one table a little boy in a baseball cap in animated discussion with Mom in shorts and thongs and Dad in a Hawaiian shirt; at another, two elderly ladies delightedly deliberating over what to choose for dessert.

I swim in a motel pool. I have only just begun to swim again and at first it felt as if my arms would tear off at the scar tissue. Now in the small pool my stroke reaches out, relaxed and steady. Heading home, I stop for a picnic lunch on a quiet Tahoe beach where Ponderosa pines shade the sand. Five self-confident Canadian geese bob among swimmers, periodically venturing onto the beach to cadge food from the sunbathers, only to be chased back to the water by giggling children. I stop briefly at a county fair in the Gold Country hills and watch the furious competition of a cake decorating contest in which an elaborate wedding cake and a castle come enchantingly to life. I return gratefully to the cool air of the Bay Area, triumphant with what I have done.

*   *   *

Two or three weeks after the end of radiation, I hit the skids. Ordinary life feels assaultive. I can't modulate how much is coming at me and it keeps coming. One area is the business of living—phone calls, car trips, arrangements, things breaking down. Annoying in ordinary health, depleting in this time.

About the same time I have several special social events that I've been looking forward to, but they all come the same weekend and the weather turns suddenly hot. I care about these people and many are greeting me for the first time since the cancer. The exchanges are warm, the talk meaningful. Suddenly without warning, I am overwhelmed by the noise, heat, and sheer intensity of interchange. For ten months I have visited with people mostly one on one, in quiet surroundings. Now I have unleashed my full social personality, and it is more than I can handle. Feeling the conflict between my social self on the one hand and the limitations of my body and the person who has lived in a cocoon on the other, only heightens my distress. Once I identify all these stresses and alter my approach and expectations, I do better in another, smaller group. This time I stay in a quieter inner place and let myself feel the gap between me and the growing energy, speed, and multiplicity of conversations. What a breathless, complex sport! Gently I touch the small pincushion-centered, metal portacath still imbedded under the skin near my left shoulder. It was real--not just a dream--that netherworld of being hitched up to chemo-therapy. Released now, I sit here, a bit dazed, but centered in my present place. I inhabit a curious limbo somewhere between portacath and buzzing sociability.

*   *   *

I tap another cause of distress. As I listen inside my body, an image forms of my hands over my head, trying to protect myself from bombard-ments. This is what the last couple of weeks have felt like. Then I make an intuitive leap. This isn't only about the excess of ordinary life right now. It is also the beginning of feelings about what I've been through in the past ten months bubbling to the surface. It is about the assault of the news of cancer, one piece of nasty news on top of another, one surgery after another, one treatment after another, one hospital stay after another. It is about the intense focus to keep centered and surviving under the rat-a-tat fire of events.

Now emerges the image of a shell-shocked veteran. The war is over, but inside his head, his experiences keep replaying and he can't yet relate to the world to which he has returned.

Because of past experiences, I knew there would be emotional pieces to pick up after the crisis was over. Sometime in the spring, I had an image that I might feel like a person who had been kidnapped, taken on a long bumpy ride by threatening captors, and then, one day, dumped by the roadside. She is grateful to be alive and rid of the kidnappers, but has to pick herself up, dust herself off, and find her way home. Now I am in the confusing process of finding my way home, and home is not the same. I am not the same.

Once these images have come to match the emotional experience, my distress ebbs. But the fatigue and difficulty of finding a comfortable level of activity remain. Fatigue now makes even my morning routine of walking and meditating before shower and breakfast exhausting. I don't tolerate sun or heat and there is more of both. Sometimes it's hard to tell how much of my debility is physical, how much emotional, and how they intertwine. This is a time requiring utmost gentleness toward myself, knowing that my ongoing low energy can stir up my critic. The Accomplisher-Doer-Critic wants forward movement and, discomforted, turns on me.

*　　*　　*

I go to do a spot of therapy and am helpfully reminded of making the distinction between forward movement and level of activity. I *am* engaged in forward movement; for now my level of activity and expectations need to be modest. I opt to use the rest of the session to do a sand tray, a Jungian therapeutic activity in which one selects from a vast array of little human, animal, and imaginary figures and natural and man-made settings to create a tableau. This activity tends to engage the concentration in the manner of a child purposefully at play. At first I choose a couple of animals just because they appeal, then I see an alligator, the creature that came as a dream symbol of the first cancer. I feel my aversion to it, then in a flash, I take the offensive, pick up the alligator, and set it in the center of the sand tray.

After that, my hands reach for pieces as if knowing what they want: an operating table, on which I set the alligator, assorted male and female medical figures, and spiritual-healing and wisdom figures--a witch, a Buddha, a totem pole, a wizard--and finally, a knight in armor, astride a charging horse. I know his lance is for the alligator, but how will I get it to penetrate?

I turn the alligator over, and see that its head is articulated at the neck, leaving a little open space at the throat. I lay the alligator on its back on the operating table, its vulnerable belly exposed, and thrust the knight's lance deep into the throat. I breathe a deep sigh as I gaze at the image of this last year's work. It makes a dramatic tableau, but it is not finished. The edge on which I'm living now is not yet represented. I pull an arched bridge off the shelf, and set it at the foot of the operating table. On the bridge, I place a stretcher holding a wounded soldier. Good: there's my war-torn veteran on a bridge to something else. I cannot know what that something else will be or who I will become, but I want an image that suggests potential for the future.

Hanging out on the edge of the scene are *The Wizard of Oz* characters: the Cowardly Lion, the Tin Man, and the Scarecrow. I selected them at the beginning, when I was picking out things that appealed to me without yet seeing a relationship. Now I know they belong at the far end of the bridge that holds the wounded veteran. These characters set out on a voyage, hoping to find a cure to their afflictions. It led them to change how they viewed their disabilities and to find a way to live more comfortably in the world. Right now I feel uncomfortable, unable, and enormously vulnerable in an unfamiliar world. I will need to create a new relationship to myself and the world as they did. For now I put a friendly arm around my vulnerability and remind myself to honor it.

*   *   *

On a morning walk in mid-August, I feel the grumpiness, fatigue, and discouragement that have been building in me. To break my obsessive head chatter, I ask inside, "What's between me and feeling good right now? What would I need in order to feel okay?" The answer breaks through: "Energy!" Then comes the reluctant admission: for now, I need to accept this fatigue. I listen for what else is there. I'm alive. I've come through a lot and come through well. That's true, but it doesn't help the way I feel now. I am still full of grumpiness and. . . . What? *Resistance.* Yeah! *My body doesn't want to move on.* I feel downright uncooperative. For ten months I've worked hard. Does Life say, "Wowie! Good work! Take a bow. Take a rest."? It does not. Well, listen, Life. I don't like your way of dishing it out. You're about as cozy and personal as a bureaucracy. Yeah, come to think of it, *I don't like your style of relating.* And boy, I've had dose upon dose of having to cooperate. *I've had it up to here*!

Well, whaddaya know. Welcome, Anger Honey! I've been wondering all through this when you'd come out in full force. I notice you keep a low profile during crisis so more serviceable parts can run the show. But now that you're here, give me all your energy. Open up my diaphragm, oil my vocal chords, tune my voice, and put plenty of air in my lungs. Are you ready? Let's go!

You stinker, Life. You stinker, for sending me that nasty, rotten cancer!

*　　*　　*

Although this letter ends with this incident in August, my cancer story is certainly not finished. The journey of emotional recovery is an integral part of it, and that journey has just begun. Without external structures and procedures, obvious purpose and drive, this phase differs from the era of treatment. It is a muddlesome time of balancing rest with gradual return to old activities and thoughts and tryouts of new ones. It is a time of some pleasures and of appreciation for being alive, but also of feelings of flatness and blocked energy broken by surges of anger, grief, and fears for the future.

I rather expect that one more letter may be necessary several months from now. Judy, the writer, may need to aid Judy, the post-cancer patient by chronicling the convalescence of the war veteran and the voyage of discovery of the Tinman, the Cowardly Lion, and the Scarecrow on their way to Oz.

Love, Judy

Dear Reader,

Mentally I've titled this letter "The Hardest, The Worst, The Best, The Proudest, The Learningest: Where am I now? A Glance Toward the Future." It's a letter I think could be particularly useful after treatment is over, but you may find some of the questions and ideas helpful at the end of whatever you mark as a stage. Many mini-markings might even be a strategy of coping and a heartening way of seeing your progress.

So this is an invitation to look back at getting cancer or at a particular phase of treatment. What was the hardest part? Are there benefits it has brought? What makes you feel proud of yourself? What learning has come out of the experience? Are there changes you want to make in your life based on things you've learned? Are there new things you want to muse about doing, even if you're not yet ready to do them?

Any of these questions could feel threatening as well as inspiring, so address only those that are right for you at a given moment. I'm going to offer you some safety aids for this activity. Then I'll share what was hardest for me, what scares me still, the benefits I derived from getting cancer, what makes me proud, and what I learned.

Some Safety Aids

Knowing you have the complete privacy of your journal or a pad of paper may give you freedom. On the other hand, you may feel that safety lies in having company. Perhaps suggesting this topic for discussion or writing in a support group will give you a sense of sharing a voyage; you could also do it with another cancer patient or a friend who wants to explore the questions in relation to another issue. Even if you want to share some of your writing or discuss the issues aloud, you can choose to keep any part for yourself alone. And remember, you determine comfortable boundaries if something feels threatening. You can even explore in writing, before you approach your material, what those boundaries are.

If you're looking back to a painful phase in the past, imagine yourself as the person who lived through that time, much as you can look back to the vulnerable child you were, who can now be comforted and healed by your adult understanding. As with the child that you were, you can now put an arm around or hug or receive the tears or anger of the person who went through all that. If you're looking at something painful in the present, you can also reach out to the part of yourself that's in pain.

If you find you're judging yourself, acknowledge the presence of the critic and use any of the techniques I suggest in the letter about the critic. If your critic won't step aside, work with it. Another tack is simply to list the facts of the painful topic or describe the situation as though you were talking about someone else's crisis. Do you or did you judge your own handling of the situation the same as or differently than you would if it were someone else?

Possible Approaches

Take any one of the following categories and just list whatever comes to mind. If you find you are thinking about more than one category, set out several pieces of paper each with a heading such as: "The Worst," "The Hardest," "What I'm Proud of," "What I Learned," "What I'm Afraid of," "The Benefits," "Where Am I now?" "Changes I Want to Make," "Ideas for the Future." Then just list whatever comes to mind on the appropriate sheet. You may find yourself adjusting the titles or adding new sheets. The idea is to get down as many possibilities as come to mind, without going into detail on this first round. You might find that some item belongs under more than one heading. That, in itself, may make for fruitful exploration. For instance, something that was very hard may also have brought a benefit.

If feelings emerge about what you're writing down, you can tell them you'll come back to them soon, but for right now you just want to make a list. Another way is to name the dominant associated feeling or contradictory feelings beside each entry. *You may well have contradictory feelings!* Writing down the names of accompanying feelings is a good way to keep them from working covertly! For instance, if it frightens you that cancer brought a benefit, such as getting a lot of nurturing and attention, you may fear that you need cancer in order to have that benefit, and if so, does it mean you are courting cancer in the future?

The act of writing down such a fear is a first step in lessening its power. For that particular issue, you can ask at any point, "How might I get a similar benefit or that need met now or in the future?" Or you can just keep such a question in mind as a safety feature, telling the list or the feelings that you will later brainstorm possible solutions. When making a list of the benefits, you will probably find that some continue in you as positive self-development—new skills, new external resources, new confidence. It's as important to spend time with positive findings as with the bumpy places. By all means, toot your own horn and revel in your "copability" and smarts!

Another approach is to explore the first item that comes up or lures your attention as you go along. But if you choose to make a list, you may find that just doing that has given you something unexpected. You may want to write about or take time just to feel fully what that is. Seeing my own list gives me a sense of the balance and wholeness of my experience and the richness of my ability to cope. You may now or later look at the list and see if there is one item that you want to explore in writing or with another person. If you go on a writing spree, keep in mind some of the things I've suggested in other letters: expressing, receiving, and being with whatever feelings come up; imagining yourself made up of a variety of parts and feelings. If one part is in pain, is there another that could help comfort and heal it? Remember that you can let a feeling or a part speak. You can also talk to it or write it a letter.

If you are reading this following treatment, the subject "Where am I now?" may be particularly pertinent. In the aftermath, you may feel yourself changed. You or others may assume you can go back to business as usual. Yet your energy may be low or unreliable and your emotions bouncing around. You may not feel like your old self and be wondering who this new self is. Remember that your cancer treatment has been an important, probably central activity for an extended time. Now you have lost both the adreneline and single-minded purpose of treatment. Yet your reality is not what it was before you were diagnosed, even if you have been able to keep up some of your usual activities. It might help to see this as a transitional phase. In my mind, it is as much a part of dealing with cancer as treatment is. It may be a time to re-read the letter on the fear of loss of self and muse on what your particular issues of self-identity are right now.

The questions, "Are there things I want to change in my life?" and "What about the future?" might also be useful so long as you don't put pressure on yourself to come up with immediate solutions or changes that you may not be ready for yet. You might view this as a gestation time for new ideas or plans. It took a full year before I was ready to act on my idea of offering writing groups for cancer patients. Some changes may have to do with looking at ways to reduce obligations. If you feel a need not to take on everything you were doing before cancer, this could be a time to assess that.

Here are the lists I made when I first sat down to start this letter. As I write, it is almost exactly two years since the end of my treatment. My list is not in any particular order, just however things that came to me over a period of several days. This activity might be of interest more than once, as your list could alter with time.

The Worst, the Hardest

Learning I had cancer again.

Meanings I feared it suggested about my chosen lifestyle. Was what was vitally important to me bad for me?

Interrupting the writing of my first book.

Threat to my value of personal growth.

Fear for my life.

Losing my breasts, especially the nipples.

Getting pneumonia.

Losing my hair.

Back trouble and weight gain induced by reduced physical activity.

Being often shut in, with less access to the world, less mobility.

Being dependent on John.

Intensifying our problems of both working at home in limited space.

The offered possibility of the then very new, experimental bone marrow transplant.

The bone marrow biopsy, bone marrow harvest, and the chemo that followed the bone marrow harvest.

Subtracting more from my sexuality.

What still scares me

Fears of recurrence: fear for my life, fear of cancer interrupting writing this book.

The Best

Contact with people from all parts and eras of my life.

Weaving relationships with new people, medical and other.

Writing the cancer letters.

Positive response to me and my writing.

The response making me trust to open up and share more, making me a better writer.

Readers—sometimes people not known to me—sharing their personal journeys and meanings with me.

A much higher proportion of enjoyable personal mail than usual!

Loss of large breasts benefitting my back.

Emotional efficiency—not getting bogged down in the little complaints I'm more likely to get sidetracked by in ordinary life.

Creating a sense of community, which I believe others felt as well as I.

Receiving generosity.

Appreciating that I was helping to bring out the best in myself and others.

Full access to my sense of humor.

Living creatively.

Appreciating John's and my ability as a couple to keep working posi-
tively with the conditions imposed on us.

Appreciating our different skills and John's devising a system for
medical bills and talking endlessly with insurance and business/
office people.

Appreciating John's steadfastness.

His appreciation of the way I "just packed the bag and went back in
over and over again to the next hospital surgery, the next hospital
chemo."

Ongoing and Resulting Benefits

Not having to wear a bra anymore.

Regaining my hair with all its previous curliness and wave and increased body.

Having a publisher, so I'm not isolated in my writing.

All the new people who are now part of my life.

The Learningest, the Proudest

Seeing how well the long inner work I'd done served me in crisis.

A much clearer view of my abilities both as a person and a writer.

Experiencing a new level of self.

Where am I now?

Here with you!

Reaching out to you as people reached out to me.

Affirming the power of community.

Wanting to end by saying, "Count me among your cheering section.
Take heart. Hang in there!" I send you lots of healing energy.

Love, Judy

October, two years later

Dear Friends and Dear Reader,

It is now exactly two years since I wrote the last letter to my friends. I have just completed the ten letters to you, the reader. It is time to bring you together.

Dear Friends, let me introduce you to the reader, a person we didn't know existed when I was fighting cancer—someone who is full of possibility and interest and who may be battling for health as I had to battle.

Dear Reader, let me introduce you to my friends. As they participated in my healing and I experienced them as a community, I now offer the power of their presence to accompany you on your journey.

May these introductions enlarge your sense of connection to each other and to life itself. We never know what small encounter may bring us something we need.

And now I want to complete my tale of the aftermath of cancer treatment and the journey toward emotional healing.

*   *   *

I end the last letter to my friends with the fatigue, anger, grief, and bumps that are part of the post-treatment era. They continue through the fall and even off and on into the winter and spring. Sometimes it is hard to know how much is physical, how much is emotional, and how much one exacerbates the other.

I have a run of uncharacteristic events: losing my checkbook, my normally reliable car having a flat tire on the highway, then twice for unrelated reasons breaking down and having to be towed, once from a town forty miles away. Finally rested from the exhaustion of these demanding inconveniences, I recall the fantasy deal I made with the universe when I felt overwhelmed after seeing the bone marrow doctor: trading my situation for the annoyances that make us grumble in ordinary life—difficulty finding parking places, standing in line, and so on. So, Universe, now that is behind me and I am successfully through treatment, you are calling me to honor my part of the contract!

To help ride out this uncomfortable phase, I seek out quiet, nurturing places. I find myself frequently returning to the botanic garden in the park. I sometimes sit on the same bench where I stopped on that eery afternoon before my mastectomy, not yet aware that it was an earthquake that had caused me to lose my balance on my walk along the ridge. I go to visit an old school friend in Washington state, who lets me sit and stare at the peaceful lake outside her windows. I work on my last letter in another friend's cabin in the Sierras, where the one loud sound is made by deer browsing outside the window. Nature is an important healing resource.

I try a breast cancer post-treatment support group in the hospital, run by a couple of my nurses. But I have to go to the meeting room up on the Oncology floor with all its sensory reminders, and the discussion is largely about Tamoxifen, which only burdens me with the memory of not even being a candidate for that non-toxic, ongoing protective treatment. "Such nice people," one voice in me says to quell my resistance to returning, "and they won't always be talking about Tamoxifen." But I have to trust the voice in me that says it isn't right for me at this time and go my way.

I take a gentle movement class that *is* just right. The easy, fluid motions and sounds that well from inside bring forth fresh emotional meanings. My body expresses its held experience of treatment and allows me to shed tears and to comfort it and the Judy who went through all that.

By November I begin to feel more in balance. With the help of a friend, I hang in my new study a flying black and gold carved wooden Asian horse—a zesty, magical symbol of my creative energy. I get my "College of Radiation Oncology" diploma framed in bright red, ready to hang, once I buy the furniture for the new room.

In December I tap a feeling of being on the run and afraid to stop. I ask myself, "What would happen if I stopped?" The answer comes: "I'm afraid the cancer will catch up with me." Once that connection is made conscious, I ease, knowing I can separate my pace of activity from fear of recurrence. Another December hurdle: my oncologist moves his practice to join the group of oncologists in the hospital. Not only am I ripped away from the staff whom I've come to know in his old office, but now I have no choice: I have to go back into the place that has negatively conditioned me with so much trauma.

I wait for blood work in a room full of people receiving out-patient chemo. Having had my chemo as an in-patient, I've never had the mass experience and it is affecting. It's the same room (now organized for a different use) where I had the bone marrow biopsy. A bowl of fruit on the table beside me commands my attention as someone talks with a patient about food and eating. A wave of chemo-conditioned nausea whooshes through me. Yikes! I've heard about this, but never had it since treatment was over. A nurse points me to one of the beds now available, where my turn will come for blood work. As I lie down, I get a whiff of the bed linens, one of the primary smells now associated with chemo. My nausea and light-headedness intensify. I catapult off the bed and return to the chair by the offending bowl of fruit. When the nurse returns, I tell her what is happening. She takes me to a chair in an adjoining room for my blood work, and I think, How am I going to be able to tolerate coming here from now on?

In January I go to a professional to do some deconditioning hypnosis. It is so successful that when I return to the hospital for my monthly appointment, I have no physiological reactions. Nonetheless, I tell the nurse and doctor about my prior experience, enlisting their aid, should it happen again. While my blood is being drawn, I catch sight of a chemo pump stashed in a corner. I hold it in my gaze and stare it down as one would turn and face a bully and watch him wither. I walk out of that hospital triumphant. I have regained one part of it as a friendly, non-toxic place, and already I'm beginning to weave relationship with the warm, kindly staff.

Also in January I feel the first stirrings that I may soon be ready to tackle writing a book proposal. It is too soon to start my writing group for cancer patients—I'm still riding my own ups and downs. Emotional and physical recovery form an organic process that cannot be pushed.

Then I hit a rough patch: our VW Bug is stolen again. I feel my vulnerability loop back to the cancer—the suddenness, the irrevocability, the instability of life.

In February and March I do a slow, thorough job of weeding out things for an "At Home Sale and Social" for friends and neighbors. I exchange the old for the new. The proceeds buy me a hand-crafted writing table. The party/sale and resulting table make people I love part of my nascent study, where the cancer letters they received will become a book that reaches out to others as friends reached out to me. I acknowledge both the increased physical capacity that allowed me to put on the event and my extreme fatigue.

One Saturday morning in May, I am mystified when I can hardly hold my arm up to wash my hair in the shower. When I get out, I see that the entire arm is swollen. My doctor, mercifully on duty that day, asks me to meet him in his hospital office. Suspecting a blood clot caused by my portacath, he escorts me down fast-route back stairs and delivers me for a venogram. I, who was on my way to a Kentucky Derby party in San

Francisco that day, whirl inwardly at being once again co-opted by emergency. Blood clot confirmed. The result: one week in the hospital on intravenously delivered blood-thinning medication, the first twenty-four hours in the Intensive Care Unit.

My body responds like the trooper it is and everything goes well, but as I am wheeled to the Oncology floor to spend the rest of the week, I wonder whether it will cause chemo-conditioned nausea. After all, I'll have to live snuggled up to the #!*<@ smell of those sheets, the @#$%<*\ pervasive odor of the soap in the bathroom, and other less definable olfactory displeasures of *that place.* To my surprise, none of this is a problem. The hypnosis and face-the-bully encounter of several months ago have really done the job. (Nonetheless, to this day I have an uneasy relationship with the hospital soap, which I occasionally run into in other public restrooms, and avoid using, so the smell won't linger on my hands.)

This episode turns out to be an unexpected gift of emotional healing, not only for me, but for my nurses. They don't often see one of their patients return to this floor looking so well. Although I know I will have to continue on blood-thinning pills for some months to come and next week will have the portacath surgically removed, the major anxiety is over.

When I get home, I hit the skids and assume it is due to being suddenly exposed to a heat wave and noisy street work right outside our normally quiet house. My back, which went into spasms from so much bed rest, and the torn-up sidewalks make even a little walk difficult. I feel more trapped than in the hospital, where at least it was cool and quiet and I could walk down long, flat corridors. I talk with a friend on the phone. Smart in the ways of the psyche, she says gently, "It sounds as if you did what you were so good at during the cancer: finding and creating the most positive experiences in a tough situation. But how do you feel about having surgery next week—being cut again?" She adds her own shuddery sound, "Ouuuu."

"You're right: Ouuuu," I acknowledge. "I don't want to have another surgery—not even a nothing-to-it one."

"Having a blood clot, even if caused by something that can be removed, must have been scary. Might have even triggered a fear of dying."

Bingo. I feel a big shift within me. "Yeah! So that's the major cause of this distress. I was terrified in that initial emergency. And I *was* afraid of dying. Then once things were on the okay route, I settled in to cope with the week in the hospital. That poor old fear got stashed." Feeling the release, I talk now about the fear, and when I hang up, I know that irritating as this combination of back, heat, and street noise are, they will pass. I've come out of the twilight zone.

The surgery is minor. The once helpful, now offending portacath is out. (If you are a portacath user, don't waste a lot of worry about this happening to you. It doesn't happen often, but if it should, I hope my account will reassure you that it's not as bad as your fears, which are natural.)

By June I have a sense of being born into a new era. I'm ready to try out a different post-treatment support group, and now the timing is right for me. I go for several months and enjoy contact with a core of people who come regularly, some of whom sign up for my first writing group.

In July, one year after finishing treatment, I offer my first writing group for cancer patients and post-treatment vets. I am now comfortable being with other cancer people and I experience great pleasure in retrieving my teacher self and connecting to people professionally.

In October I have the excitement of being interviewed by three different TV stations for Breast Cancer Awareness Month. In the midst of calls about program-airing changes, comes the never-to-be-forgotten Oakland Firestorm, two years almost to the day from the 1989 earthquake and my mastectomy. Our house is not in the path of the fire, but the uncertainty and enormity of the situation remind us of the earthquake/ cancer year. As John and I monitor the fire's direction on television, we are reminded of watching television on the evening of the earthquake. When we turn it off, I say, "The only good part is that at least I don't have to go for a double mastectomy tomorrow morning!" And while I feel the vulnerability of our whole community and have yet to make many calls to verify the safety of friends, the link to the vulnerability of cancer is less. Time *does* make a difference.

October ends with a contrasting bit of delight. I am invited to be a judge of the employees' Halloween costume and pumpkin contest in the cancer center. What greater honor could fortune shower upon me! As I move with my high-status clipboard through an area of patients who have been enjoying the creative dress of their medical staff, I say, "I'm one of you! Look at what glory awaits you when you finish chemo!" Only one man looks at me as though I've been let out of a mental institution against sounder judgment.

I weave anti-cancer activities and images into my daily life. I walk every morning and swim as often as possible. I balance the disciplined work on this book with time in nature, visits with friends, and nourishment for my inner child. A day at a rubber stamp festival does wonders for her!

Every morning I do a twenty minute meditation. I no longer follow exactly the prescription I was originally given, because over time I felt too regimented, and doing exactly the same thing every day became onerous. I do sit down daily to do some form of meditation. I usually settle in by doing a few minutes of visualization or/and affirmations. I'll hit on something I like and do it for as many days as it lures me, then let something else emerge. Sometimes I imagine millions of French shopkeepers, who sweep in front of their stores every morning, clearing away any unhealthy cells, then pouring buckets, not of ordinary water, but of a liquid of my healing green color throughout my body.

Sometimes I name the most crucial parts of my body in relation to cancer, then imagine the sweepers at work, ending by pouring green liquid throughout my bloodstream, my lymphatic system, my bones and bone marrow, my liver, and my lungs. Sometimes I'll name as many parts and organs of the body as I can think of and then, like a child who has named loved ones in her prayers and asks God to bless anyone she has forgotten, I add "and all the other body parts I don't even know."

Other times I simply imagine every single cell in my body being inspected and any irregular ones thrown out and incinerated or transformed into healthy ones.

I also make and repeat affirmations. My favorite one these days is: *My cells are healthy; I am healthy.* I have even turned this sentence into a kind of chanting mantra.

A friend asks if I'm eating lots of broccoli. Well, I eat some, but I confess, forcing myself to eat more of it would stir up my inner rebel. But her mention of broccoli makes me think of a rubber stamp I have of dancing vegies. Now I invite Broccolettes and Broccolettos to dance through my entire body, releasing their anti-cancer broccoli essence into every cell.

At some level, the awareness of cancer is always with me as are fears for the future. They can be triggered by something another cancer patient or veteran says or by hearing of a cancer death. They are most likely to be aroused by people who discuss treatments and want to know if I am taking Tamoxifen, or eating my broccoli, or following any particular regimen. Oh dear, I think, I probably really should look into that. Then I retrieve my own inner space and know that I have my own idiosyncratic dance of life.

In April, about twenty months after finishing cancer treatment, I go through one stressful five-week period after a CA 15-3 tumor-indicator blood test registers higher than ever before. It is still just within the normal range, and doctor, lab tech, and nurses all remind me of the flightiness of the test and that one time doesn't tell the story. It is rerun a month later rather than waiting the usual two and comes down to a number of unimpeachable respectability. Living with the anxiety sometimes caused by this frequent and quirky test is one of the legacies of my particular cancer.

In August I go on a week-long Focusing retreat and, to my surprise, find that my work is taking me into cancer issues. In one session I note a discomfort in my throat and chest, which I assume is purely physiological—a touch of heartburn from the unaccustomed breakfast of walnut pancakes! But when I seek a word to describe it, what comes is *raw* and an unexpected association with chemotherapy, followed by tears and comforting the Judy who had to go through all that. Emotional healing is continuing in its own time and ways.

In another Focusing session, I tap one place of vulnerability and another of vitality. Though the vulnerability first relates to my back, my association quickly leaps to cancer. "I *never, never* want to have cancer again," I say, and spend some time just being with that feeling. What comes next for me is a wish that I could reassure myself that I never will have it again. Acknowledging that I am like a parent who cannot guarantee that no illness will befall her child, I ask myself what the parent *can* do when something bad happens to a child. The answer comes: Take care of it and offer lots of love. I did that very well for myself through cancer and I would do it again if anything adverse were to befall me. My fears and worries about recurrence ebb, and I spend time with the place in me that feels my aliveness.

The next morning I have dreams and take one small, fuzzy scene into my next Focusing session. In this dream I find two old tickets to a concert, somehow connected to a friend who was killed in Vietnam. The dream is suffused with bittersweetness and surprise at coming upon a forgotten memento of my youth. The tickets go back to a time before my friend went to war, a time of innocence and trust. As I stay with the emotion of the dream, I experience myself retrieving the trust of pre-cancer innocence. As I feel the power of that returning trust, suddenly this sentence bursts forth: *It is finished.*

I say the sentence aloud over and over in a voice of wonder, because "it" seems to refer to cancer now and in the future. *It is finished. It is finished. The cancer is finished!*

Back in ordinary awareness, my logical left brain says, "Of course there are no guarantees." But that experience strengthens my ability to believe in my ongoing freedom from cancer. That gift from my unconscious and my body helps me to let go of worries for the future. It is inevitable that they come from time to time, usually when I'm worried about something else. When they do come, I try to get clear on what the something else is, and I go back to that powerful emotion of *It is finished.*

* * *

As I prepare to leave you, I send you my very best wishes for your life and healing journey. And when you hit a rough patch and feel at your wit's end, see if it helps—even a little bit—to imagine putting an arm around the hurting you and offer yourself lots of love. And here, once again, is mine to you.

Love, Judy

Appendix 1

Breathing Exercises to Reduce Anxiety and Increase Comfort

When highly anxious, we're likely to breathe shallowly, sometimes even holding our breath for short intervals. The cumulative effect of shallow breathing intensifies both anxiety and physical discomfort. Attending to our breathing can help open it up again, which in turn calms anxiety and increases physical comfort. These breathing exercises will serve you in moments of crisis, when you feel much too agitated to consider subtler psychological techniques or approach a problem thoughtfully. They may also increase feelings of well-being when you are limited in mobility. Once you experience the benefits, you may invent your own variations, but here are some techniques that should bring significant relief.

1) Deep breathing: Take a long, slow breath inward through the nose, then let it out slowly through the mouth or nose. If you continue to do this for several minutes, you will notice some physical quieting, probably accompanied by a reduction in anxiety. You can anchor your attention in a variety of ways: count slowly with each inhalation and see what number you reach comfortably and if it's the same on the exhalation; see if the top number stays the same or increases gradually as you continue. You may find that your breaths become more regular or longer and slower. When that happens for me, I notice a reduction in chaotic feelings. Try putting your hand on your diaphragm and feel it swelling. The more

space opens up in there, the more ease you'll feel. You can mentally repeat a word like "love" or a phrase like "I am safe" to accompany your breathing. Invite imagery to form. It doesn't have to be anything madly creative! I often imagine my breath coming not in a straight line up from my diaphragm, but in a line that curves front to back like this: Ƨ

Following that curving line in and out focuses my awareness in a calming way. If you prefer, you can consciously choose imagery—animals, people, colors that are comforting for you, a peaceful spot, a picture of yourself being held, protected, or cared for, an image of healing—whatever holds your attention, even momentarily.

2) Alternate nostril breathing: Hold the left nostril shut with your left thumb and breathe in slowly through the right nostril. Then simultaneously release your thumb, cover the right nostril with your left index finger, and exhale slowly through the left nostril. Breathe in through the left nostril, then release your finger from the right nostril, cover the left nostril with your thumb, and exhale. Continue alternating and feel free to use your other hand, other fingers, or whatever arrangement is most natural and comfortable for you. You can do this in a public place, sitting casually, elbow on chair arm or supported by your other hand or wrist, with your chin more or less in or against the hand from which you sneak a finger to the side of your nose. You're just looking meditative, like someone with chin in palm.

3) Taking a deep breath and letting it out slowly through a slightly

open mouth during any specific procedure that makes you anxious can be helpful. I have long done this for my back before lifting something, getting up off a medical table, and so on, to reduce strain, and I usually did it for needle procedures and when I anticipated even minor pain. It gives you something to do and, by a deliberate relaxation, counters the tendency to tighten muscles. When my oncologist moved from his practice to join the cancer center in the hospital, he cheerfully advised that I warn my new nurses of my idiosyncracies. "To which of my unique and sterling qualities are you referring?" I asked, composing my body to its full dignified stature. "The way you breathe that sounds as if you're in cardiac arrest when having your portacath flushed." Admittedly this letting out of breath, unlike the alternate nostril technique, is a noticeable sound. If it makes you feel less self-conscious, by all means clue in your medical helpers. They're likely to be impressed that you have such savvy. My oncologist's remark may make you wonder whether you can trust my assessment that you can do the alternate nostril breathing unnoticed in public. Oh, go ahead, try it, and see! As a skilled practitioner, you may recognize someone else who has read this book doing it and strike up an anxiety-reducing conversation, or make a friend for life!

5) Breathing with sounds. For this one you do need privacy or under-standing fellow dwellers. It is the most effective technique I know for high anxiety. I do it for a good ten minutes or more. I lie on the living room floor, but do whatever is comfortable for you. Breathe in slowly through

your nose, then exhale slowly through your mouth, while making a sound. I find the "O" sound (similar to the Eastern meditational "Om") brings the fullest calm and relief, so I usually do a lot of that, especially for the first few minutes while establishing an even rhythm and increasing the resonance. But you can experiment with all the vowels, even diphthongs, and "Om." You can also change sounds and pitch in the course of an exhalation. For example, "ooh, aah, eee." Your voice may rise or fall a notch or slide continuously up or down in the course of any sound or as you change from one sound to another. Doing so makes for variety, attention absorption, exercise of facial muscles which can feel enlivening, and sometimes humor. You may even begin to play with sound in a childlike way or deliberately squinch different parts of your face. I do not recommend that you do this one in public, unless you can get a whole bunch of people to agree on it as a group activity—and warn any innocent non-participants!

6) Singing is also a very good way of increasing your air intake without thinking particularly about breathing and could give you pleasure in itself. It can help the sluggishness that comes from forced lack of exercise. If you don't think of yourself as a singer or don't know many songs, try recollecting ones from when you were young or ones you've sung with your children. I sometimes go back to songs in French and Spanish I learned in school. With repetition, the "da-da, da-da's" gradually get replaced by the full set of words, and I feel quite refreshed by the time I've finished.

Appendix 2

Cancer Resources

Your hospital or oncology or radiation oncology department probably has a social worker who can offer you immediate emotional support as well as practical information about other resources. There are also hundreds of cancer organizations and support groups across the country and in Canada. Look under "Cancer" or "Health Services" in your Yellow Pages directory or contact any of these national organizations for their offerings and information about what is available in your area.

NATIONAL GROUPS

The American Cancer Society (ACS)
1599 Clifton Rd. NE
Atlanta, GA 30329-4251
(800) ACS-2345

Calling this number reaches your state division of ACS. If you have a local branch, it is usually listed in the phone book as American Cancer Society of (your county). They or the national 800 number have lists of local support groups and a resource particular to breast cancer called "Reach to Recovery." You can be paired with a trained volunteer, a person approximately your age, whose cancer and treatment were similar to yours, and who will talk on the phone and visit you.

National Alliance of Breast Cancer Organizations (NABCO)
1180 Avenue of the Americas, 2nd Floor
New York, NY 10036
(212) 719-0154

A central source of information and an advocate for legislative and regulatory concerns. Customized packets, resource list, and quarterly *NABCO News* for members.

National Black Leadership Initiative on Cancer
Los Angeles, CA
(800) 262-5429

National Breast Cancer Coalition
P.O. Box 66373
Washington, D.C. 20035
(202) 296-7477

The coalition educates the public about breast cancer advocacy and, through its national alert network, provides ways for individuals to become actively involved in the fight to stop the breast cancer epidemic.

National Coalition for Cancer Survivorship
1010 Wayne Ave., 5th Floor
Silver Spring, MD 20910
(301) 650-8868

Information on "survivorship"—from diagnosis onward for the rest of life: especially psychosocial issues such as anxieties within family, about recurrence, insurance, employment discrimination, and long-term side effects. Newsletter,

The Networker, and other publications. Annual conference of survivors, supporters, and medical caregivers.

National Coalition of Feminist & Lesbian Cancer Projects
P.O. Box 90437
Washington, D.C. 20090
(202) 332-5536

The coalition represents a growing number of organizations dedicated to the empowerment of grass-roots women's cancer groups and is committed to working together for changes on a national level. The groups offer a variety of support services, education, and political activity. Contact with the coalition is through The Mautner Project for Lesbians with Cancer, whose phone and address are listed here.

Susan G. Komen Breast Cancer Foundation
Dallas, TX
(214) 450-1777

The Wellness Community National
2190 Colorado Ave.
Santa Monica, CA 90404-3504
(310) 453-2300

Free psychosocial support: support groups for patients and their families, education, social events; all geared toward helping people fight for recovery along with medical treatment. Eleven groups around the country at time of publication, more being developed.

Y-ME
National Organization for Breast Cancer Information & Support
18220 Harwood Ave.
Homewood, IL 60430
National Hotline, 9-5 weekdays for information and support:
(800) 221-2141
24-hour Emergency Hotline: (708) 799-8228

Wide range of information: treatment options, referrals, support groups, advocacy; and services: pairing with volunteer who had your kind of cancer and treatment, wig and prosthesis bank, newsletter, reading list and lending library.

Resource information also for Canadians, including location of support groups, and the 800-number is accessible from Canada.

INTERNATIONAL GROUPS

AUSTRALIA

The Breast Cancer Support Service
Queensland
(07) 257-1155

CANADA

The Alliance for Breast Cancer Survivors
20 Eglington Ave. W., Suite 1106
Toronto, M4R 1K8, Canada
(416) 487-9899

A proactive survivor-directed organization, working to promote the partnership of survivors, funding agencies, government, and those concerned about breast cancer to bring about better prevention, treatment, and education. Information on Canadian support groups, newsletters, resources, telephone networking.

Breast Cancer Action Montreal
Montreal, Quebec
(514) 276-4575

Burlington Breast Cancer Support Services, Inc.
Burlington, Ontario
(416) 634-2333

The Canadian Cancer Society
10 Alcorn Ave., Suite 200
Toronto, Ont. M4V 3B1, Canada
(416) 961-7223, weekdays, 9-5 eastern time
(or consult local unit listed in your phone book).

Public education, research funding, and patient services carried out by volunteers aiming to enhance the quality of life for people with cancer. Support groups for patients and their families; "Reach for Recovery" one-on-one program pairing new breast cancer patients with women who have had similar cancer and treatment. Prostheses available for temporary use without cost. Some provinces have lodges at reduced rates for patients who have to travel a great distance for treatment. Arrangements to reimburse for drugs not covered for patients who can't afford them.

NEW ZEALAND

Breast Cancer Support Society
affiliated with the Cancer Society of New Zealand
Auckland
(09) 524-0023

Federation of Women's Health Councils Aotearoa-New Zealand
Auckland
(09) 520-5175

PUERTO RICO

Preventing and Surviving Breast Cancer Project
Taller Salud, Rìo Piedras
(809) 764-9639

UNITED KINGDOM

Breast Care & Masectomy Association
London, England
help-line: (071) 867-1103
main number: (071) 867-8275
Glasgow, Scotland
help-line: (041) 353-1050

Women's Nationwide Cancer Control Campaign
London, England
help-line: (071) 729-2229
main number: (071) 729-4688

* * *

Coping
2019 N. Carothers
Franklin, TN 37064
(615) 790-2400

A bi-monthly magazine for people living with cancer, published by Media America, *Coping* offers a cancer survivors' guide and a variety of articles of interest to anyone who has or has had cancer.

Support Groups

If you are considering a support group or have just tried one and have mixed or negative feelings, it may help you to know that the character of support groups differs from one to another. Some of the difference lies in the leader(s) and the chemistry of the participants. But groups also emphasize different things and are better at some features than others. For instance, some may be led by oncology nurses or other medically knowledgeable personnel who are particularly good at responding to your technical and medical questions in a leisurely, non-threatening atmosphere. This setting can be especially helpful if you feel too rushed or timid with your doctor, or simply if another source of information about other women's experiences with a drug or treatment could broaden your understanding and offer comfort.

Some groups may be especially good at receiving your feelings, helping you express and work with them, and may be led by someone with a degree in clinical psychology or social work. Others may be interested in the political ramifications of breast cancer and related political activity. Some groups identify themselves specifically as feminist or/and lesbian. Some are led by former cancer patients with training and experience in leading groups. Groups may be for all cancer patients or specifically for women with breast cancer, for during treatment, for post-treatment, or for people with metatastic or recurring cancer. They may be open to family members of the patient, or the same organization may offer separate support groups for family members.

All are legitimate kinds of groups, but it may help if you know what focus most interests you. Just being aware that there are different memberships, styles, and approaches may help you ask questions ahead or assess the benefits and discomforts of a particular experience. All support groups have the potential for providing the comfort of being with other people who are in the same boat, and for having your anxiety raised for the same reason. If you want a group, but are not comfortable with one you just tried, another one may be just the ticket. You may also want to consider being paired with a trained volunteer who has been through your kind of cancer and will be there for you as a knowledgeable insider.

Appendix 3

Other Emotional Support Resources

Healing and Relaxation Tapes

The following tapes are of exceptional quality, made by professional therapists with extensive experience and skill in the use of imagery and open-ended positive suggestions to promote healing. The tapes are sensorially pleasing, complex, and interesting so that the listener will not tire of them quickly, and they hold up to coming back to again and again. Having several tapes allows you to rotate them.

Tapes made by Belleruth Naparstek, M.A., L.I.S.W.:

Barry Rothschild
Image Path, Inc.
P.O. Box 5714
Cleveland, OH 44101-0714
(800) 800-8661

Titles particularly pertinent to cancer: Cancer, Chemotherapy, Depression, Surgery, Grief, General Wellness. Side one of each tape is guided imagery that juxtaposes suggestions for both physical and emotional health against a background of gentle music. Side two has affirmations. The surgery tape has music to take into surgery on one side. The General Wellness tape could be useful after the end of treatment, when you really don't want to hear any more about cancer and chemo, but want to continue healing messages.

Tapes from the Erickson Institute

Made by Carol Erickson, L.C.S.W., M.F.C.C. and Thomas Condon, M.A.
Erickson Institute
P.O. Box 739
Berkeley, CA 94701
(510) 526-6846

These emotionally supportive, relaxing tapes have more general uses than physical health. Some titles particularly relevant to cancer patients: Sleep, Pain, Self-Hypnosis, Self-Confidence, Quick Stress Busters. Tapes are "double induction": a powerful and pleasing technique of interweaving voices. Tapes include music and some other relaxing sounds.

* * *

Focusing

The Focusing Institute, Inc.
29 S. LaSalle, Suite 1195
Chicago, IL 60603
(312) 922-9277

You can get the name(s) of Focusing teachers in your area or perhaps someone who might travel to you to give a class or workshop. Once you learn Focusing, you will have access not only to other classes and workshops, but to pairing with a Focusing partner or joining a free "Changes" group where members share Focusing sessions on a regular basis.

Focusing Books and Manuals

These books and manuals may be of interest, not only if you want to learn the skills they teach, but even if you don't feel up to taking on an active learning process and just want to spend time absorbing kindly, supportive, healing ways of being toward yourself, your experience, and your feelings.

241

Focusing
Eugene Gendlin, Ph.D.
NY: Bantam Books, 1981

A general introduction to Focusing with directions on how to do it. Gendlin observed what successful psychotherapy clients were doing inside themselves and put together a way to teach the skill, which he called Focusing. It is useful not only in psychotherapy, but also for approaching any life problems and the full range of emotional experience.

Let Your Body Interpret Your Dreams
Eugene Gendlin, Ph.D.
Wilmette, Il: Chiron Publications, 1986

Good for beginner and experienced alike, it offers ways of looking at dreams—and ourselves—and many open-ended questions to help unlock meaning.

The Focusing Student's Manual
Ann Weiser Cornell
Focusing Resources
2625 Alcatraz Ave., #202
Berkeley, CA 94705
(510)-654-4819

A step-by-step guide used in Focusing classes. These constantly updated manuals are well laid-out, with clear, comprehensive directions and large print.

* * *

One Last Resource

The Chemotherapy Survival Guide: Information, Suggestions, and Support to Help You Get Through Chemotherapy
Judith McKay, R.N. and Nancee Hirano, R.N., M.S.N.
Oakland, CA: New Harbinger Publications, 1993
How chemo works and how to prevent, minimize, or cope with side effects written by two oncology nurses with contributions by a physician, a nutritionist, and a clinical social worker. Discusses nausea, fatigue, hair loss, nutrition, blood tests, I.V.s, support groups, stress reduction, and offers a script from which you can make your own healing visualization tape.

Conari Press, established in 1987, publishes books for women on topics ranging from spirituality and women's history, to sexuality and personal growth. Our main goal is to publish quality books that will make a difference in people's lives—both how we feel about ourselves and how we relate to one another.

Our readers are our most important resource, and we value your input, suggestions, and ideas. We'd love to hear from you—after all, we are publishing books for you!

*   *   *

For a complete catalog or to get on our mailing list, please contact us at:

Conari Press
1144 65th Street, Suite B
Emeryville, CA 94608
(800) 685-9595